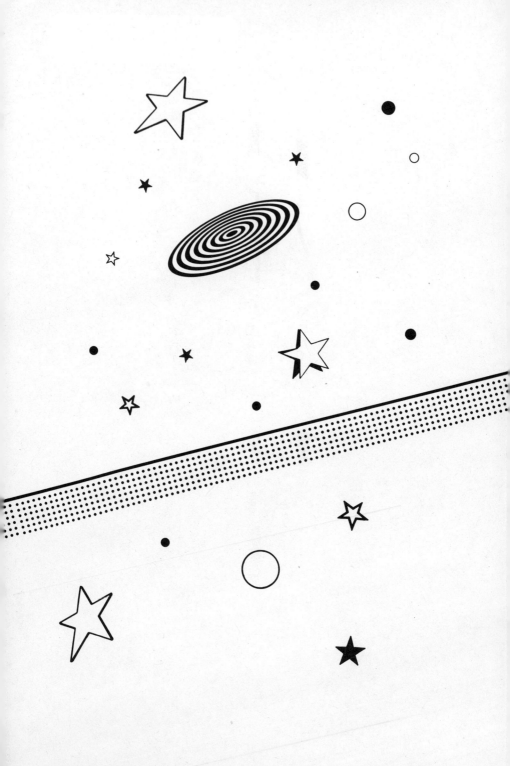

F.L.Y.E.R.S.™

Fun Loving Youth En Route to Success

Lawrence Graham

&

Lawrence Hamdan

Illustrations by Gerry Shamray

A Fireside Book
Published by Simon & Schuster, Inc.
New York

A Fireside Book
Published by Simon & Schuster, Inc.
Simon & Schuster Building
Rockefeller Center
1230 Avenue of the Americas
New York, New York 10020

FIRESIDE and colophon are registered trademarks of
Simon & Schuster, Inc.

FLYERS and "Fun Loving Youth En Route to Success" are registered trademarks of FLYERS Consulting and are used with their permission.

Designed by Levavi & Levavi
Manufactured in the United States of America

1 2 3 4 5 6 7 8 9 10

Library of Congress Cataloging in Publication Data

Graham, Lawrence.
    F.L.Y.E.R.S. : fun loving youth en route to success.

    "A Fireside book."
    1. Youth—Anecdotes, facetiae, satire, etc.
2. Young adults—Anecdotes, facetiae, satire, etc.
I. Hamdan, Lawrence. II. Title. III. Title: FLYERS.
PN6231.A26G73 1985   818'.5402   85-14468
ISBN: 0-671-60369-8

Acknowledgments

Lawrence H.: Now let's make sure we thank everybody.

Lawrence G.: That's right. We can't let it be said that FLYERS aren't grateful. Where should we start?

L.H.: At the tippy-top, where else? With Martin Davis at Gulf + Western who put us in touch with the wonderful people at Simon & Schuster: Richard Snyder, Cathy Hemming, Barbara Gess (our editor), our promotional wiz Julia Knickerbocker, Herb Schaffner, Judy Lee, Chris Lloreda, Jennifer Kittredge, Stacey Holston, Janis Vallely, Torrey Paulson, Florence Falkow, Jean Rodriguez, Dan Chiel, Jeanne Palmer, Eve Kirch, Patty McKenna, Deborah Bergman, and their phenomenal sales force.

L.G.: And what about all those special people who've helped us out, like your brother Allen Hamdan and my brother Richard Graham, our fantastic lawyer Paul Blaustein, the entrepreneurial James A. Grasfield, our illustrator Gerry Shamray, Tyrell Holston, Patricia Manzone, George Atwood of Delta Tau Delta fraternity at Tufts University, Diane Bessette, Sharon DeLevie, Paul Boghosian and Ken Eisenstein at my lecture agency, Steve Emanuel, Mark Muro, Lila Colburn, Ted Higgins, Mary Van Lawrence, Kimberly Wheeler, Nina DeLuca, Teresa Nevola, Jordan Horvath, Leslie Fagenson, Tufts University, our business clients of FLYERS Consulting, and our nationwide network of student testers?

L.H.: We can't forget all our friends at Harvard who lent a hand: Dauna Williams, David Billings, John Copeland, Mark Duesenberg, L. Elise Dieterich, Amy Chua, Andrew Gordon, John Moylan III, Jason Abrams, Anthony Farley, Carol Degener, Brad Roth, Donald Green (for all the magazines we borrowed), and our study group partners David Jones and David Schwartzbaum.

L.G.: And all those FLYERS at Tufts: Karen Pattani, Simon Ringrose, Brian De-Broff, Elizabeth de Givenchy, Paul Foldi, Alex Jackson, Eve Dubrow, Cathleen Marine, Dexter Congbalay, Deirdre Lowe, Ann Marie Cannistraro, John Kirk, Andrew Cohen, Ruth Patkin, James Dopp, and John Drayton.

L.H.: And we just have to thank Dante Implicito, Jeff Gordon, Bud Pygon, Mike Karpa, Tim Milway, Gerry Lally, Jerry Hoehn, Mike Geiger, Tom Geraty, Al Dalcourt, Mike Gibbons, and all our other FLYERS friends at Harvard, Princeton, Wellesley, Mount Holyoke, Lesley, Berkeley, Johns Hopkins, Duke, UCLA, Texas, Michigan State, Chicago, UVA, Columbia, Notre Dame, Beloit, St. Bonaventure, U. Mass., Seton Hall, Tulane, and Boston College.

To
Betty & Richard and Dorothea & Ali

Contents

WHO THEY ARE

GENERAL LIFESTYLES

SOCIAL LIFE

CAMPUS LIFESTYLE

EMPLOYMENT WORLD

THE BIG PICTURE

Who They Are

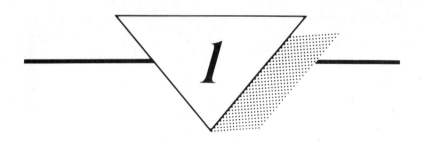

How FLYERS Define Themselves

FLYERS (flī′ərz), n. 1. acronym for "*Fun Loving Youth En Route to Success*" (yes, we know we skipped over the word *to* but as easy-going FLYERS we didn't notice until it was much too late to do anything about it—and who'd want to be called a FLYERTS anyway?). 2. Any outrageous, carefree, crazy, hilarious, wild, high-spirited people who are oblivious to past problems, live the present at full blast, and expect (deserve) only the best from the future (sounds appealing, don't you think?). Antonyms—Nerd, Geek, Social Donut, Yuppie, Dweeb.

"Are you now or have you ever been one of the FLYERS?" If you're still not sure after that incredible definition, here are a few more details:

FLYERS expect inevitable success. They're not overly paranoid about the world blowing up tomorrow. How could you even make *next* weekend's outrageous party plans with confidence? FLYERS know that the budget deficit isn't nearly as bad as having to miss a good rock concert (in fact, the tremendous national debt gives FLYERS an excuse to overspend, since they wouldn't want to show up the U.S.

government). You just can't be secure about your future, or even enjoy a 50-keg bash, if you're waiting around for the next international catastrophe to come along.

FLYERS are quick to claim their independence—even if they're still claiming an allowance. Just like they can't be forced to eat liver and Brussels sprouts, they can't be coerced into the Terrifying Threesome of Marriage, Homeownership and (oh, the horror!) Yuppiedom.

FLYERS pride themselves on their individuality—even if they do all wear Levi's and wild T-Shirts; spoil their dinners with the same junk foods; wait on endless lines to see the same rock concerts; stay up late to watch "Saturday Night Live", "The David Letterman Show" and the same TV comedy reruns; etc. Still, Eddie Murphy fans respect the rights of Clint Eastwood fans, and vice versa. FLYERS can buy both Madonna and Prince records with ease. And they will accept you into their group whether you wear your Vuarnet sunglasses over your eyes or in your hair.

Overall, FLYERS have an intense time wherever they happen to be—and you just might be one yourself (if you're lucky!).

2

FLYERS Tip #1:
How to Remain Oblivious to the Arms Race, World Hunger and other Current Events That Can Put a Damper on Your Bright Future

Every FLYER knows that the secret to success lies in his or her ability to maintain a high I.Q. (Ignorance Quotient) on events taking place in the outside world. If you can ignore world-wide crises and forget past disasters, you'll be able to get on with the more important things in life, like arranging your weekend-party schedule, shopping for new clothes, or hanging out with friends at the mall.

Test your ignorance with the FLYERS I.Q. Test and make sure you don't know more than is necessary. Although the questions get easier as you go down the list, a true FLYER will draw a blank on each one!

The FLYERS I.Q. Test

1. **During which century did the Vietnam War take place?**
2. **What very tall U.S. President with a beard is honored by the Lincoln Memorial?**
3. **Which item do starving countries need most of all?**
4. **Name the American city where the Chicago Fire took place.**
5. **In what year did the "Crash of '29" occur?**
6. **In which country is the Japanese yen used as currency?**

A Typical Day in the Life of FLYERS

MORNING AND AFTERNOON: 6 A.M.–5 P.M.

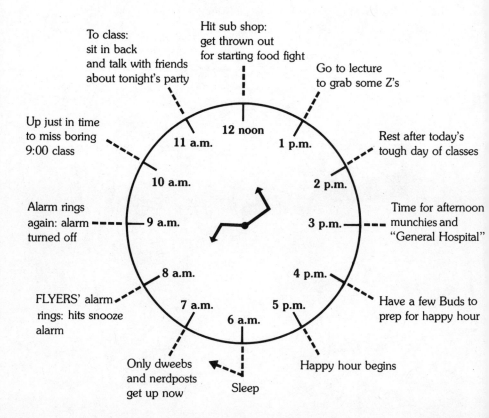

To class: sit in back and talk with friends about tonight's party

Hit sub shop: get thrown out for starting food fight

Go to lecture to grab some Z's

Up just in time to miss boring 9:00 class

Rest after today's tough day of classes

Alarm rings again: alarm turned off

Time for afternoon munchies and "General Hospital"

FLYERS' alarm rings: hits snooze alarm

Have a few Buds to prep for happy hour

Only dweebs and nerdposts get up now

Sleep

Happy hour begins

11 a.m.
12 noon
1 p.m.
10 a.m.
2 p.m.
9 a.m.
3 p.m.
8 a.m.
4 p.m.
7 a.m.
5 p.m.
6 a.m.

EVENING: 6 P.M.–5 A.M.

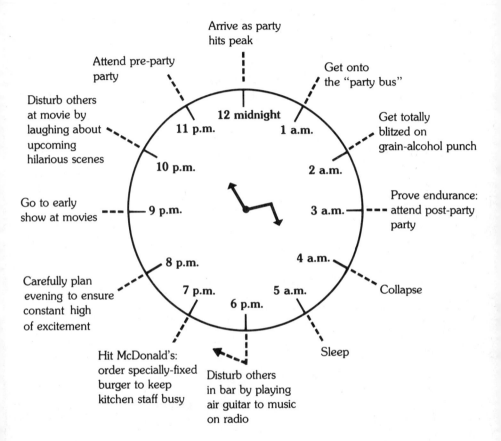

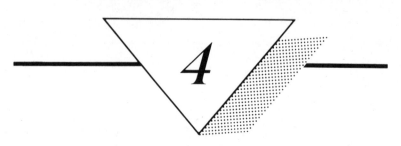

Well-Known FLYERS
Under Age 25

JENNIFER BEALS—Even if she's got only a little acting experience, the fact that she could make a sexy movie like *Flashdance* and go to Yale at the same time proves she's one of us. And don't forget that off-the-shoulder sweatshirt look—just perfect for FLYERS who don't have the time to make sure their clothes fit.

SEAN PENN—His line, "Hey bud, let's party" in *Fast Times at Ridgemont High* has become a FLYERS motto.

TOM CRUISE—His role in *Risky Business* (where he gets sex, money and a college acceptance in two short hours) shows FLYERS the way to live.

TIM HUTTON—Listen, if he's got the talent to win an Oscar at his age, he's got to be one of the most talented FLYERS in the biz.

JOHN KENNEDY, JR.— Even though the Kennedy mystique guarantees John-John a place in this FLYERS list, he has already had quite a few professional achievements all on his own (although we're not entirely sure what those achievements are).

SAMANTHA SMITH—By giving up international diplomacy (she wrote a letter to the Soviet leader and was invited to visit Russia) and going to Hollywood to star in a new sitcom, Samantha made the glitzy choice all FLYERS would.

DOUG FLUTIE—This Heisman Trophy winner signed a contract for millions, millions, millions. In spite of all the hype, hype, hype, he is amazingly cool—just as most FLYERS would be in the face of so much money and media attention.

CORNELIA GUEST—Debutante of the Year 1981. If you haven't heard of the lovable and glamorous Cornelia, where have you been? Born of socialite parents, she has achieved a balanced FLYERS lifestyle by heating up the hottest dance clubs and livening up any party she hosts or crashes.

MICHAEL JORDAN—This Chicago Bulls guard is the only man who can fly without a reservation. His jumping ability doesn't hurt his popularity with the fans either.

LAWRENCE GRAHAM & LAWRENCE HAMDAN— that's us, the authors of this book. (Modesty is not a FLYERS virtue.)

Sixteen Things FLYERS Would Never Be Caught Dead Doing

Because FLYERS are a much envied group, one has to be sure that one's friends are on the level. To assure yourself that those around you are true FLYERS and not just cheap copies, use the following checklist of non-FLYER characteristics.

FLYERS Would Never:

1. Iron a crease into a pair of Levi's
2. Attend a Donny Osmond concert
3. Send away for the blueprints to the "Star Trek" *Enterprise*
4. Plan a career in mechanical engineering
5. Beg their parents to let them join the Boy Scouts
6. Break up with a steady date and then agree that they were to blame
7. Arrange a dentist appointment without being coerced
8. Order clothes from an L.L. Bean catalog
9. Raise hybrid roses as a summertime hobby

"Do you think anyone from school will recognize us in these disguises?"

10. Agree to go on a blind date—without first seeing a head to toe photograph, or without being paid

11. Go to the beach in order to go swimming

12. Ask their parents about birth control

13. Open a birthday card that contains no money, and conclude that it's the thought that counts

14. Finish an assignment for a boss or teacher before it's actually due

15. Lose sleep over the national deficit

16. Clip food coupons to help save on shopping

6

The FLYERS Eat-or-Remember Board Game

FLYERS have managed to incorporate soda and junk food into almost every aspect of their lives. By playing this amazingly innovative game, you and your friends can test yourself on FLYERS trivia while also filling yourselves with fun and tasty snacks.

The Rules Go Like This:

1. Before you and two or more friends begin the game, starve yourself for eight hours.

2. Collect the following *Ingredients for the Game*:
   —1 box of Hostess Twinkies
   —3 packs of Bubblicious Bubble Gum
   —2 boxes of Orville Redenbacher's Microwave Popping Corn
   —2 regular-sized mushroom and pepperoni pizzas
   —a half-gallon of Baskin-Robbins Rocky Road ice cream
   —2 rolls of Pillsbury Slice-n-Bake Cookies
   —a 12-oz. bag of Chuckles Spearmint Slices

—2 24-oz. jars of Marshmallow Fluff

—3 bags of Cheez Doodles

—a Giant size box of Good 'n Plenty

—8 Jello brand Pudding Pops

—10 York Peppermint Patties

—a 6-pack of Diet Coke

—4 Baby Ruth bars

—8 mini-packs of Goobers or Raisinets

—a can of Redi-Whip Cream Topping

—a 6-pack (any brand) of a "non-lite" beer

—2 bags of Plain or Peanut M&M's

—3 Big Macs and 24 Chicken McNuggets

—2 boxes of Fiddle Faddle

—5 chocolate-covered Klondike Bars

—10 slices of Sara Lee Chocolate Layer Cake

—a 3-liter bottle of Mountain Dew

—a dozen creme-filled Dunkin' Donuts

—2 pounds of Hershey's Kisses

—8 oz. Nestle's Quick, plus milk

—a giant-sized bag of Tootsie Pops

—a tub of Betty Crocker Ready-to-Spread Lemon-Flavored Frosting

3. Each person throws the dice to find out how many squares he or she must move.

4. When a square is landed on by a player, the player must either *eat* the food which is listed, or they must *remember* the answer to the question which is asked by that square on the board.

5. Players must watch their opponents swallow the respective articles of food before the next throw of the dice.

6. The first player to reach the final square of the game gets all of the uneaten food which was purchased for the game, as well as a free bottle of Pepto Bismol.

(board follows on next page)

THE FLYERS EAT-OR-REMEMBER BOARD GAME

START HERE

Eat 2 Hostess Twinkies or *Remember* the name of the pig that starred in "Green Acres."	*Eat* a handful of Cheez Doodles or *Remember* the date of Cyndi Lauper's birth.	*Eat* 1 slice of Sara Lee layer cake or *Remember* who won last year's Cotton Bowl.	*Eat* 3 Hershey's Kisses or *Remember* how many buttons are on a pair of Levi 501 jeans.	*Advance* **4** *Boxes*
Drink 6 oz. of Mountain Dew or *Remember* Madonna's real name.	*Eat* 2 pieces of Bubblicious Bubble Gum or *Remember* who sings the theme song to "Love Boat."	*Eat* 2 Slice-n-Bake cookies or *Remember* the full names of 5 female characters on "All My Children."	*Eat* 4 Tootsie Rolls or *Remember* what Natalie Wood was wearing when she drowned.	
Eat 1 scoop of Rocky Road ice cream or *Remember* the name of Joan Collins' autobiography.	*Eat* 2 handfuls of buttered popcorn or *Remember* who won the Heisman trophy last year.	*Drink* ½ can of Bud or *Remember* the name of Brooke Shields' college.	*30 Second Pig Out— Everybody Eats!!*	
Eat 1 Klondike ice cream bar or *Remember* last week's top-rated TV series.	*Eat* 1 creme-filled Dunkin' Donut or *Remember* the average number of chocolate chips that go into a Chips Ahoy cookie.	*Eat* 2 handfuls of Fiddle Faddle or *Remember* the names of 3 different cats, 2 dogs and a gorilla who each had their own TV cartoon show.	*Eat* 2 spoonfuls of Ready-to-Spread frosting or *Remember* who appeared on the cover of the first issue of *People* magazine.	

26

Eat 1 Jello brand Pudding Pop or *Remember* the last 2 cover stories on the *National Enquirer.*	*Eat* 6 Chicken McNuggets or *Remember* 3 TV shows which featured Sally Field.	*Eat* 2 spoonfuls of Marshmallow Fluff or *Remember* 2 songs from Bruce Springsteen's "Born in the USA."	*Eat* 1 York Peppermint Patty or *Remember* the names of 4 models who have been "Cover Girls." ➡
Eat 1 Big Mac and go back 2 spaces.	*Group Chug of Nestle's Quik.*	*Eat* 1 Baby Ruth bar or *Remember* Liz Taylor's latest boyfriend.	*Eat* 1 "spritz" of Redi-Whip cream topping or *Remember* when the Frisbee was invented. ➡
Eat 10 pieces of Good 'n Plenty candy or *Remember* the last 3 Oscar-winning movies.	*Eat* 1 slice of pepperoni pizza or *Remember* who co-starred in Eddie Murphy's latest movie.	*Drink* 1 can of Diet Coke or *Remember* and sing the theme song from the movie *Fame.*	*Eat* 1 minipack of Goobers or Raisinets or *Remember* what makes up a Burger King Whopper. ➡
Eat ¼ cup of peanut M&Ms or *Remember* the name of Clint Eastwood's first movie appearance.	*Eat* 5 Chuckles slices or *Remember* what hero resides in the basement of a house called "Stately Wayne Manor."	FINISH *Finish!!* You win all the uneaten food plus 1 free bottle of Pepto Bismol.	

27

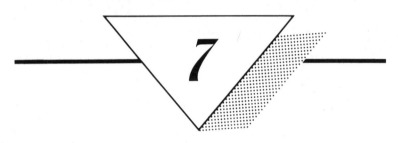

The FLYERS Theme Song

Videos, jeans, and pizza pie
Without my soda pop, I know I'd die.
Asking for allowance, oh what the heck
One day I'll earn that weekly check.

We're FLYERS!! We're FLYERS!!
I know I'll be happy and rich all the more
By flying high now and escaping the bore.
We're FLYERS!! We're FLYERS!!

Mom's not happy with the friends I date—
The discos, the shopping malls, or my coming home late.
Living the good life gives Dad the chills
But I say my future will pay all the bills.

We're FLYERS!! We're FLYERS!!
I know I'll be happy and rich all the more
By flying high now and escaping the bore.
We're FLYERS!! We're FLYERS!!

The arms race, a bad grade—I never complain.
But to clean my own room—now that's a pain.
Stereos and sports cars—there's so much to buy.
You're only young once, why wait 'til we die?

We're FLYERS!! We're FLYERS!!

Save for tomorrow—what a ridiculous rule
I've paid all my dues just by going to school.
Sitting in class day after day
Watching my social life trickle away.

Teachers and homework can be such a pest
Predicting your future with a midterm test.

We're FLYERS!! We're FLYERS!!
I know I'll be happy and rich all the more
By flying high now and escaping the bore.
We're FLYERS!! We're FLYERS!!

Junk food and beer, they're good for my health
They'll somehow contribute to my future wealth.
They say that we're wasteful, but they don't know
One day we're going to make just a pile of dough.

We're FLYERS!! We're FLYERS!!

Career, marriage, and family are things to postpone
Just live for the now—a rule I condone
Why suffer now when I can have fun?
Isn't that the reason why we stay so young?

Plans for the weekend—a movie tonight,
Our future's insured—it'll all work out right.

We're FLYERS!! We're FLYERS!!
I know I'll be happy and rich all the more
By flying high now and escaping the bore.
We're FLYERS!! We're FLYERS!!

General Lifestyles

8

Inventions FLYERS Are Waiting For

Venetian-Blind Eye Glasses

When life gets too tough, learn how to shut out the world with your very own pair of venetian-blind eye glasses. With a simple twist of the louver bar which hangs from the lens, you can avoid seeing trouble, oncoming disaster, and people that you don't want to meet.

Velcro-Covered Beer Cans

Thank goodness for Velcro! The next time your friends send you back to the bar for seconds, don't try to balance all those drinks in one hand. With velcro covers, you'll be able to grab hold of one can and stick the others on—thus carrying as many as 25 or 30 at once.

The Notebook-Skateboard

First it's a looseleaf notebook to use in class, then it's a skateboard to use on weekends. The tough canvas-covered creation has wheels on the flip side and holds up to 400 sheets of lined paper.

Mug on a Rope

For those times when you need to have both hands free. Whether you're socializing at a crowded party, relaxing in the bathtub, or riding your bicycle—you can carry this mug of beer around your neck without worrying. No more will you accidentally pick up someone else's glass, or be the unlucky one who arrives at a party just when the last paper cup has been used!

The Dorm Room Curtain-Skirt

Pull out that curtain rod and slip that belt through instead, when you turn these sunny cotton drapes into a party dress that will delight your friends. Saves money and time.

Dress-Up, Slip-On Shoe Tops

Turn your sneakers into a dress shoe for any occasion with black or brown slip-on vinyl tops which attach to your sneakers and give you that starched, dressed-up look without requiring that starched, dressed-up feeling. Each pair comes with stick-on high heels for that extra air of social sophistication (types for men and women).

A Carryall Head-Belt

Since FLYERS are always wearing shorts on the beach or on the playing field, they have the perennial problem of finding pocket space to carry keys, lipstick, wallet, etc. But with a Carryall Head-Belt, FLYERS will no longer suffer this problem.

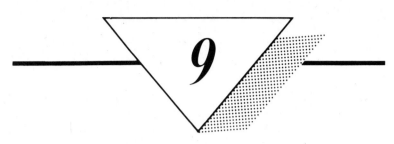

The Importance
of Nicknames

There are no typical FLYERS names. How could a parent know that one day their child would become one of the FLYERS? However, there are certain names which clearly do *not* have the right fun loving ring. Although there are no hard and fast rules, the following names are the kiss of death for FLYERS:

13 NAMES FLYERS WOULD
NEVER WANT TO HAVE

Women	Men
Agnes	Abner
Bertha	Adolph
Beullah	Boris
Brunhilde	Chauncey
Claribel	Ebenezer
Doris	Egbert
Edna	Felix
Ermengarde	Marmaduke
Gertrude	Mortimer
Mabel	Poindexter
Matilda	Rudolph
Myrna	Waldo
Winifred	Wilber

But even if you were unlucky enough to have been given one of these names at birth, don't despair. FLYERS have an easy and fun way to transform any name into a perfectly acceptable nickname.

Warning: If you have a name that needs changing, do it yourself. Better to change your name from Doris to DeDe, than to run the risk of being pegged by someone else as Dumpy Doris. And even if you have a perfectly good name, using a nickname adds to the casual, devil-may-care image that FLYERS pride themselves on. Here are five simple ways to put any name into appropriate FLYERS form:

1. Give yourself a new first name—preferably one that has some relation to your real name. For example: Poindexter becomes Dex, Gertrude becomes Gigi, Magdelena becomes Madonna.

2. Use your middle name—Your parents may have given you a first name to honor some dead relative. But they also may have given you a fun loving middle name to compensate. For example: Bertha Bunny Plotz becomes Bunny or Chauncey Blades Botnick becomes Blades.

3. Use the first syllable of your last name—(usually for men). For example: Egbert Fisher becomes Fish; Mortimer Rodriguez becomes Rods.

4. Use initials—(especially common for women). Beullah can become B. or BeBe, Matilda Josephine could be M.J.

5. Made-up nicknames— Many hardcore FLYERS take a crazy made-up nickname just to prove how fun loving they are. Examples include Snoops, Buggs, Firebird, Boomer, Blitzer, Flabs, Ace, Pippy, Belcher, Pinky, and Snaggles. To get a wild nickname, just get yourself involved in any outrageous stunt—something is bound to come up which you can use as a nickname.

10

The FLYERS Dress Code

FLYERS have very definite but quite basic ideas when it comes to clothes. In fact, the bulk of the FLYERS wardrobe can be reduced to just seven important items: jeans (easily converted into cut-offs), cords, sweats, sneakers/tennis shoes, boots, polo shirts, and T-shirts (see below for more about the complexity of the T-shirt as a FLYERS fashion). By mixing and matching these basic items and adding a few accessories (sunglasses, painter's cap, trendy jewelry, etc.), FLYERS have been able to create their own distinctive style. To be sure you won't violate any of the stringent dress code rules, take this FLYERS fashion quiz:

1. What is appropriate school-time wear for female FLYERS?
   a) purple polyester pants suit.
   b) a dress worn by the model on this month's cover of *Cosmopolitan*.
   c) a blouse with a Peter Pan collar and a wraparound kilt.
   d) jeans (501 or designer), brightly colored polo shirt, Ray Bans in hair.

2. *True or False*: Sunglasses are always an appropriate clothing accessory, summer or winter, day or night.

3. When attending the next meeting of the feminist society (dress is always casual), you might wear a T-shirt saying:
   a) How can I love you if you won't lie down?
   b) How can I tell you I love you when you're sitting on my face?
   c) I think I could fall madly in bed with you.
   d) Don't take the name of God in vain or She'll be very angry with you.

4. *True or False*: Wearing unmatched earrings is a significant violation of the FLYERS dress code.

5. What should male FLYERS wear for an informal date?
   a) bifocals, light blue cardigan, starched white shirt, black high water pants, white socks and black loafers.
   b) powder blue tux, maroon bow tie and dark blue shoes.
   c) bright pink button down shirt and lime green pants.
   d) cords, Hawaiian shirt, hiking boots, painter's cap with beer logo.

Answers:

Question 1: (d) is correct although (b) is a close second choice (the Peter Pan collar in choice (c) should have been a tip off to the FLYERS code violation).

Question 2: True, of course.

Question 3: (d) is correct although it would be interesting to see what would happen if you went with a shirt with choice (b) on it.

Question 4: This is a tough question and only fashion-conscious FLYERS are likely to get it right. For female FLYERS, the answer is False (it is "in" to wear unmatched earrings). For male FLYERS, the answer is unclear but probably True (it's better for male FLYERS to wear a single earring or two matched earrings or no earrings at all).

Question 5: (d) is the correct answer (if you picked (c) keep reading this book—it may help you lose your bad preppy habits).

But a high score on this quiz won't guarantee success among FLYERS unless you can prove your expertise in T-shirt selection. The following charts should help you out.

9 Favorite Things Found on a FLYERS T-Shirt

*Outrageous Statements
Such as "Pardon Me, But You've Obviously Mistaken Me for Someone Who Gives a Damn."

*Macho/Sexy Statements
Such as "I'm Not Perfect But Parts of Me Are Outstanding" or "Hockey Players Do It With Big Sticks."

*Bright, Colorful Geometric Shapes and Patterns
Yeah, yeah, it sounds punk. But it's actually that "just back from the beach" look, which can make you seem tanned even in the middle of winter.

*Anything in Chinese Lettering
When FLYERS want to seem cultured. Especially favored if it is an outrageous/sexy saying.

*School Names
Especially good if you don't even go to that school since it shows you have lots of friends in lots of places.

*The Name of the Hotel or Resort Where You Spent Spring Break
Lets your friends know that you didn't stay home preparing for final exams.

*Favorite Products
Especially beers.

*Any One-of-a-Kind T-Shirt
Proves that you will go to great lengths to get something unique to liven up your wardrobe.

*Any T-Shirt Which Has an Exciting Story Behind It
It doubles as clothing and a conversation piece.

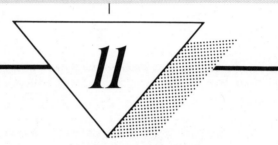

11

How FLYERS Budget Their Own Money

FLYERS have never believed the lie that the best things in life are free. When was the last time anyone was giving away rock concert tickets, a sports car, or even a free turn on a video game? In fact, many *horrible* products aren't even free, such as school books, liver and Julio Iglesias albums.

FLYERS know that if they do make out a budget, they might have to face the catastrophic dilemma of choosing between cutting down on their weekly quota of choc-olate crunch bars or not buying the newest shade of Cover Girl lip gloss.

Remaining oblivious to your bank balance is the only way to really enjoy throwing away your money on a whim. To assure that you don't even know about your budget problems, just follow these 12 handy (FLYERS tested and proven) money management tips:

DO assume that you always have more money in the bank, even if you *don't* have a bank account.

40

DON'T take time from your busy social life to keep track of how much money you have. (It takes too long to do it right—and, as everyone knows, if you can't do something right, it's better not to do it at all.)

DO ask your parents for their credit cards every time you go shopping. (You never know when they'll have a momentary lapse of good judgment.)

DON'T ever pay for anything your parents might conceivably think is essential, or that you can make them think is essential. (For example, try "I know that I could get an A+ on my term paper if I just had the information in this week's *National Enquirer*.")

DO throw away your monthly bank statement unopened—no news is good news.

DON'T ever buy something tomorrow that you can get your parents to buy you today.

DO apply for as many department store credit cards as you can. You never know when a computer error might result in them actually giving you one.

DON'T ever record withdrawals from your bank account by *subtracting* the amount from your bank balance. Subtraction is too tough to do correctly anyway.

DO record withdrawals from your bank account by *mistakenly adding* the amount to your balance.

DON'T even consider paying a bill until it's more than three months overdue. They don't really begin to threaten you with arrest until then.

DO round off numbers upward to the nearest hundred to make the adding easier when making a deposit to your bank account. (For example: You deposit $12.79, you round it to $100.00 and record that simple round number in your bank book.)

DON'T ever spare expenses when it comes to having fun. You can always cut back on nonessentials like balanced meals, school supplies, and presents for your brothers and sisters.

How FLYERS Budget Their Parents' Money

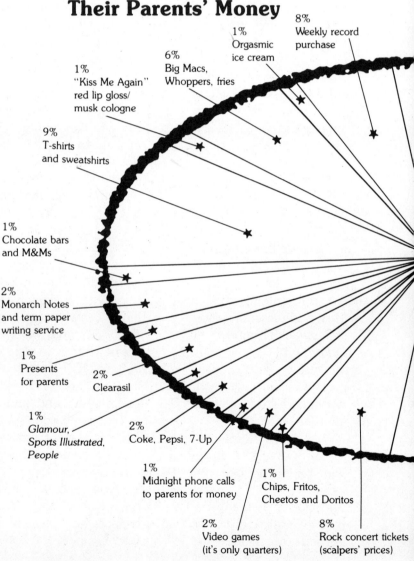

8%
Weekly record
purchase

1%
Orgasmic
ice cream

6%
Big Macs,
Whoppers, fries

1%
"Kiss Me Again"
red lip gloss/
musk cologne

9%
T-shirts
and sweatshirts

1%
Chocolate bars
and M&Ms

2%
Monarch Notes
and term paper
writing service

1%
Presents
for parents

2%
Clearasil

1%
*Glamour,
Sports Illustrated,
People*

2%
Coke, Pepsi, 7-Up

1%
Midnight phone calls
to parents for money

1%
Chips, Fritos,
Cheetos and Doritos

2%
Video games
(it's only quarters)

8%
Rock concert tickets
(scalpers' prices)

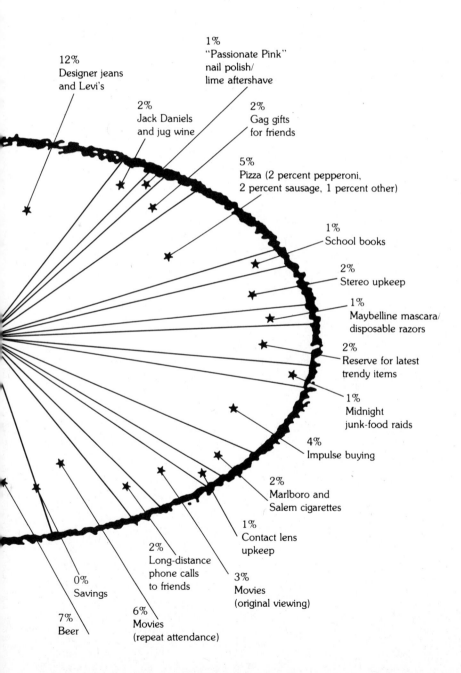

12%
Designer jeans
and Levi's

1%
"Passionate Pink"
nail polish/
lime aftershave

2%
Jack Daniels
and jug wine

2%
Gag gifts
for friends

5%
Pizza (2 percent pepperoni,
2 percent sausage, 1 percent other)

1%
School books

2%
Stereo upkeep

1%
Maybelline mascara/
disposable razors

2%
Reserve for latest
trendy items

1%
Midnight
junk-food raids

4%
Impulse buying

2%
Marlboro and
Salem cigarettes

1%
Contact lens
upkeep

3%
Movies
(original viewing)

2%
Long-distance
phone calls
to friends

0%
Savings

7%
Beer

6%
Movies
(repeat attendance)

FLYERS' Favorite Movies

FLYERS are the most faithful moviegoers. But you won't catch them paying to see Meryl Streep's newest cinematic triumph, or waiting in line for a psychologically compelling Fellini masterpiece, or sitting through any thought-provoking foreign or domestic film (why be forced to think when you're not getting graded?). FLYERS just want to feel good when the lights come up. Here's a list of the flicks that FLYERS flock to:

1. **Animal House**—Brought real respectability to the food fight. A tribute to John Belushi's ability to play a serious dramatic role.

2. **Fast Times at Ridgemont High**—Proves FLYERS love to do crazy things even when it's not for a sorority or fraternity initiation.

3. **Anything with Eddie Murphy**—(except *Best Defense*).

4. **Risky Business**—Proves that FLYERS get what they deserve (student turns family split-level into a whorehouse, then gets into Princeton).

5. **Purple Rain**—Prince and Appolonia—the perfectly adjusted FLYERS couple.

6. **An Officer and a Gentleman**—As far as female FLYERS are concerned, it had action and Richard Gere, romance and Richard Gere, drama and Richard Gere, and Richard Gere, too.

7. **Flashdance**—FLYERS love how Jennifer Beals got star billing for this movie even though someone else did most of the dancing.

8. **Footloose**—Glitzy and trashy—just down-to-earth FLYERS entertainment.

9. **Rocky Horror Picture Show**—A good excuse to sneak toilet paper, rice, and water pistols into a movie theater.

10. **Revenge of the Nerds**—Proves that even some nerds can become FLYERS.

11. **The River**—The movie is boring, but female FLYERS love to see Mel Gibson on the big screen.

12. **Star Wars**—Rumor has it that it's a great movie if you're stoned.

13. Anything by Monty Python—Early proof that there are British FLYERS.

14. **Places in the Heart**—Ever since her days as the Flying Nun and Gidget, FLYERS have always supported Sally Field.

15. **Raiders of the Lost Ark**—Just a few typical days in the lives of some adventure-seeking FLYERS.

16. **Porky's**—Raunchy and crude, but credited with increasing the average viewer's sex drive tenfold.

17. **Ghostbusters**—Shows that earning a living can be fun.

18. Any Clint Eastwood movie—He's as tough as FLYERS come.

19. **Friday the 13th** and *Halloween*—Substantiate the claim that nothing is too stupid or disgusting for FLYERS.

20. **Caddyshack** and *Stripes*—Starring Bill Murray—a favorite overgrown FLYER.

21. **Rocky**—Proves that FLYERS can get beaten up badly but still win.

22. Any James Bond movie—(Roger Moore is the James Bond of choice.) In every one, this FLYER saves the world and, most important, has sex with a fantastic looking woman.

23. **American Grafitti**—A great way to bone up on American history.

Eating Like FLYERS

Here are some sample menus of typical FLYERS meals:

Breakfast Menu

Entrees:
- Cold pizza
- Leftover Chinese food
- Captain Crunch, Fruit Loops
- Snickers Bar

Drinks:
- Coke, Diet Coke
- Pepsi, Diet Pepsi
- Chocolate milk

Lunch and Dinner Menu

Entrees:
- Pizza, Chinese food, McDonald's/ Burger King special
- Microwave burrito
- TV dinner
- Chili dog
- Chef-Boy-R-Dee Ravioli or Spaghetti-Os
- Bag of Doritos and chocolate bar
- Two cans of Bud (liquid lunch)

Cafeteria Fare:
- Last night's mystery meat (now in a Hungarian goulash)
- Vegetable soup (last night's leftover vegetables)
- Veal cutlet patty (made of processed pork)
- Sandwich (unknown meat and cheese on stale bread)

Shopping for the nutritious FLYERS meal

Snack Foods or Appetizers
(a very brief alphabetical list)

Almond Joy	Fruit Pies	Peanuts
Baby Ruth	Goobers	Peanut M&M's
Big Wheels	Good & Fruity	Pepperidge Farm
Bubble Yum	Good & Plenty	Cookies
Butterfingers	Granola Bars	Popcorn
Cheez Doodles	Heath Bars	Pop Tarts
Cheetos	Hershey Bars	Potato Chips
Chewels	Jelly Beans	Pretzels
Chewing Gum	Junior Mints	Raisinets
Chiclets	Kit Kat	Reese's Peanut
Chocolate Chip	Lifesavers	Butter Cups
Cookies	Mars Bar	Ring Dings
Chocolate	Milky Way	Smarties
Chewy	M&M's	Snickers
Granola Bars	Mounds	Three Musketeers
Chuckles	Mr. Goodbar	Tootsie Pop
Combos	Nestle Crunch	Tootsie Roll
Dentyne	Bar	Tostados
Doritos	Oreo Cookies	Twinkees
Fig Newtons		Yodels
Fritos		

15

The 60-Second
Fast-Food Trivia Quiz

FLYERS are the largest group of fast-food consumers. There is not a fact they don't know about fast-food chains. With the following 60-second quiz, you too can brush up on some of the necessary facts that are bound to pop up during future meal-time conversations.

1. Which person is really descended from a royal family?
   a) The Burger King
   b) The Dairy Queen
   c) Mayor McCheese
   d) The Prince of Wales

2. Which fast-food chain specializes in old-fashioned fish and chips?
   a) Nathan's Hot Dogs
   b) Kentucky Fried Chicken
   c) Dunkin' Donuts
   d) Arthur Treacher's Fish-n-Chips

3. Elizabeth Taylor was accused of getting stuck in the "Golden Arches" of which famous eating establishment?
   a) Wendy's
   b) Big Boy
   c) Roy Rogers
   d) McDonald's

4. Which fast-food chain was named after a famous restaurant entrepreneur?
   a) Red Lobster
   b) The Ground Round
   c) Taco Bell
   d) Howard Johnson's

5. Where does Ronald Reagan live?
   a) White Castle
   b) Pizza Hut
   c) International House of Pancakes
   d) White House

Answers:

The correct answer to all questions is (d).

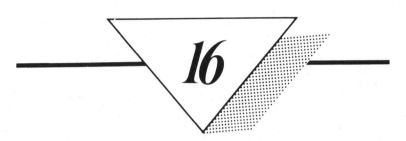

Favorite Singers and Musical Groups

FLYERS enjoy a wide range of musical styles, and lesser known regional groups are among their favorites. But among the nationally popular groups and singers, the following all exude the fun loving FLYERS image:

MADONNA (This Material Girl inspired a fashion trend of bare bellybuttons and black plastic jewelry.)
PRINCE (Let's Go Crazy over this rock sensation who rivals Madonna with his wild costumes.)
CYNDI LAUPER (Like all FLYERS, she's a girl who just wants to have fun.)
DAVID LEE ROTH (Even if he has to rip off old tunes, he has the most outrageous rock videos around.)
MICK JAGGER (With the fattest pair of lips in the business, this grand-daddy of rock is still going strong at age 40.)

TALKING HEADS (Stop Making Sense, FLYERS don't need a reason to love this wild group.)

WHAM! (During their visit to China, they tried to bring a billion more people over to the FLYERS way of life.)

TINA TURNER (Everyone loves a comeback, especially FLYERS.)

SHEILA E. (Like all FLYERS, this girl wants to lead the Glamorous Life.)

ZZ TOP (FLYERS are wild over their crazy beards and sunglasses.)

RUN/D.M.C. (These wild rappers are outrageous.)

THE POLICE (They're always in Synchronicity with what FLYERS want to hear.)

TEENA MARIE (Male FLYERS wouldn't mind it at all if she was their Lover-Girl.)

FRANKIE GOES TO HOLLYWOOD (Inspired the "Frankie Says Relax" T-Shirts—and they don't sing too bad either.)

LOS LOBOS (When FLYERS want an ethnic twist to their music.)

U-2 (Listening to their music is an easy way for FLYERS to keep up with current political events.)

THEY THINK THEY'RE FLYERS—
BUT THEY'RE NOT

BOY GEORGE (He tries too hard to seem weird. And Cyndi Lauper is a better dresser anyway.)

DURAN DURAN (For the pre-teen set only; all of their songs sound the same.)

ROD STEWART (No one thinks he's as sexy as he thinks he is.)

17

The Convertible
vs. the Stationwagon:
How FLYERS Pick Their Cars

1. The only acceptable car colors for FLYERS are: Metallic Red, Metallic Blue, Metallic Green, Metallic Gold, Metallic Silver, Metallic Orange, Metallic Cream, Metallic Brown, Metallic Salmon, Metallic Aqua, Metallic Crimson, etc.

2. Though more costly, a convertible is definitely superior to a hardtop. If you can't afford a convertible, get a T-bar roof. If you can't afford one of those, get a sun roof. If you can't afford one of those, get a hacksaw and cut a hole in the roof yourself.

3. Tinted windows are a must if you want to ignore the rest of the world.

4. Stationwagons and minibuses should be avoided, not only because they look uncool, but also because your friends will rightfully accuse you of having borrowed the family car.

5. Although some FLYERS buy foreign cars, most FLYERS prefer the domestics since they come stocked with more buttons, more knobs, and more switches to work those oh-so-necessary electrical options.

6. Cruise Control is a must. It lets you talk to your passengers and listen to the radio without that additional distraction of having to remember to keep your foot on the accelerator.

7. Your car must have an AM/FM electric-search stereo radio with at least three speakers that can

be turned up loud enough to be heard from your driveway to your bedroom (just in case your own personal bedroom stereo ever goes on the fritz).

8. Vanity license plates are acceptable as long as they don't say ambitious things like: "I LUV SCHL" or "HIGH I Q."

9. A good rule of thumb is to buy cars which are sure to get very bad gas mileage. Since you'll no doubt be using one of your parents' many credit cards, who cares about money?

10. Necessary options include power windows, power seats, power door locks, power antenna, power side-view mirror, power trunk opener, power convertible top closer (works automatically when rain drops hit the seats), and any other power option that allows you to save yourself from physical exertion.

And for those who don't want to think. . . . Here's a list of some of the *FLYERS' Favorite Cars*

1. Pontiac Firebird
2. Chevrolet Camaro
3. Ford Mustang
4. Datsun 300ZX
5. Plymouth Laser
6. Toyota Celica GT
7. Chevrolet Corvette
8. Mercury Lynx
9. Dodge Lancer
10. Pontiac Fiero
11. BMW 320i (new or used)
12. AMC Jeep
13. Pontiac Grand Am
14. Honda Accord LX
15. Ford Escort (Turbo only)

The Right Car

18

FLYERS Tip #2:
How to Set Ambitious Goals Without Scaring Your Friends

Just because FLYERS are fun loving doesn't mean they don't set a few ambitious goals in life. A FLYERS secret to setting goals, however, is to keep them under wraps. FLYERS know that the first way to lose their friends is by seeming too ambitious. Here's how to hide that ambition:

1. Before leaving your dorm room at 9 A.M. Saturday morning to go to the library, turn the stereo on full blast and leave quickly. Your friends will think you're listening to rock music all day, when in fact you're hidden away preparing for final exams in the basement of the science library.

2. If your friends accuse you of being an ambitious person, defend yourself by telling them that the only reason you work hard is because you have only two years to live, and you want to make your parents proud of you at your funeral.

3. When your roommates start telling friends that you stay up late at night to finish homework or to start extra-credit projects, start going to sleep at 9 P.M. Wake up quietly at 2 A.M. and work with a flashlight until 7 A.M. When your roomies wake up later and see you still sleeping at 9 A.M., they'll swear that you are the laziest person around.

19

The 7-Day

	Monday	Tuesday	Wednesday
2:00 P.M. 2:30	All My Children	All My Children	All My Children
3:00 3:30	General Hospital	General Hospital	General Hospital
4:00	Gilligan's Island	He-Man Cartoons	Mary Tyler Moore Show
4:30	Bob Newhart Show	Taxi	Roadrunner Cartoons
5:00	People's Court	People's Court	People's Court
5:30	Flintstones		Star
6:00			Trek
6:30	MTV	MTV	
7:00			MTV
7:30			
8:00	Bloopers &	A-Team	Simon &
8:30	Practical Jokes		Simon
9:00	T.V. Movie:	Fall	Dynasty
9:30	Animal	Guy	
10:00	House	Knots	St. Elsewhere
10:30		Landing	
11:00			Odd Couple
11:30	MTV	MTV	Carson Show
12:00 A.M.			(Guest Host: Steve Martin)
12:30	David	David	David
1:00	Letterman	Letterman	Letterman
1:30	MASH	Barney Miller	Taxi

TV-Watching Schedule

Thursday	Friday	Saturday	Sunday
All My Children	All My Children	American Bandstand	MTV
General Hospital	General Hospital	College Sports	
MASH	Bugs Bunny Cartoons		Professional Sports
Happy Days			
People's Court	People's Court		
Woody Woodpecker			
MTV	MTV	Fame	
		MTV	
Cosby Show	Magnum P.I.	T.J. Hooker	Grammy Awards
Family Ties			
Cheers	Dallas	Love Boat	
Night Court			T.V. Movie: Beverly Hills Cop
Hill Street Blues	Miami Vice	Rock Video Awards	
	The Honeymooners		
MTV	MTV	Saturday Night Live	Star Trek
David Letterman	David Letterman	MTV	
Bob Newhart Show	Mary Tyler Moore		Twilight Zone

20

Favorite Magazines

People—To FLYERS, a cover story in *People* is the second-highest honor that can be bestowed on mortal man or woman. (The highest honor is being named one of the 25 Most Intriguing People To Watch in *People's* year-end issue.)

US—More gossipy than *People* but less so than the *National Enquirer.* So it's essential reading to get a balanced perspective on important current events. Often called the FLYERS' *Newsweek.*

Rolling Stone—The magazine of choice for the pop music enthusiasts among FLYERS (especially since the giant photos in *Rolling Stone* make great posters). The magazine also includes political commentary and the examination of social trends, which make FLYERS feel more sophisticated even though they don't read these features.

National Lampoon—FLYERS love the high refinement and good taste of "The Humor Magazine for Adults"—especially the naked bosom cartoons. Will always be revered for creating the movie *Animal House.*

Cosmopolitan—Female FLYERS love the dynamic variety of articles in each issue of *Cosmo* from "You can Join the C.I.A. Too" to "Rating Your Man in Bed: A One Minute Quiz" to "Mouseburgering Your Way From the Secretarial Pool to the Executive Suite" to "My 9 Weeks as a Nymphomaniac." Much more frank about sex than the mothers of most female FLYERS.

Seventeen—Prepares female FLYERS so they will eventually be able to understand *Glamour*. Only the most mature female FLYERS can go cold turkey from *Seventeen*—gradual withdrawal is recommended.

Glamour—Delightful, enticing, fascinating, gorgeous, appealing, racy, elegant, splendid, chic, brilliant, radiant, exquisite, dazzling, resplendent, marvelous, superb—and that's just the clothing and cosmetics ads.

Sports Illustrated—The best way for FLYERS to keep up with what's happening in college and professional football, basketball, baseball, hockey, and the very popular sport of gorgeous models posing in skimpy bikinis on some island paradise.

Playboy—Sensuous literature, voluptuous articles, steamy interviews with major national figures, and arousing humor pieces are what male FLYERS drool over in each luscious, jam-packed issue.

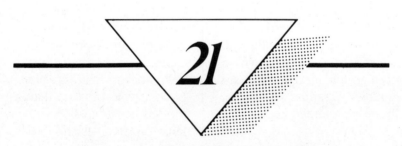

Favorite FLYERS Graffiti

Just like any group, FLYERS have their own style of graffiti. The following were discovered after a quick survey of school bathrooms and fastfood restaurants:

• PARDON ME, BUT YOU'VE OBVIOUSLY MISTAKEN ME FOR SOMEONE WHO GIVES A DAMN.

- EVERYONE NEEDS TO BELIEVE IN SOME-THING. I BELIEVE I'LL HAVE ANOTHER BEER.

- IT'S NOT WHETHER YOU WIN OR LOSE, BUT HOW YOU LOOK PLAY-ING THE GAME.

- LEAD ME NOT INTO TEMPTATION. I CAN FIND THAT ALL BY MY-SELF.

- IF YOU LOVE SOME-THING, SET IT FREE. IF IT DOESN'T COME BACK TO YOU, HUNT IT DOWN AND KILL IT.

- WE'LL GET ALONG FINE AS SOON AS YOU RE-ALIZE I'M GOD.

- I'M NOT PLAYING HARD TO GET. I AM HARD TO GET.

- THOSE OF YOU WHO THINK YOU KNOW EVERYTHING ARE VERY ANNOYING TO THOSE OF US WHO DO.

- WARD, DON'T BE SO HARD ON THE BEAVER.

- I'D LIKE TO HELP YOU OUT. WHICH WAY DID YOU COME IN?

- WHEN I WANT YOUR ADVICE, I'LL BEAT IT OUT OF YOU.

- LIFE IS TOO IMPOR-TANT TO BE TAKEN SER-IOUSLY.

- I DON'T HAVE A DRINK-ING PROBLEM. I DRINK, I GET DRUNK, I FALL DOWN. NO PROBLEM!

- I'M REALLY ENJOYING NOT TALKING TO YOU. LET'S NOT TALK AGAIN REAL SOON.

- THE SECRET OF SUC-CESS IS SINCERITY. ONCE YOU CAN FAKE THAT, YOU'VE GOT IT MADE.

22

How FLYERS Talk
to Their Parents

A father calls from his office and wakes his daughter from a sound sleep.

Phone rings. FLYER picks up receiver and says nothing.

Father: (pause) Hello?
FLYER: Who is this?

Father: Jennifer? Is that you?
FLYER: Who is this?
Father: Jennifer dear, it's your father.
FLYER: No Jennifer here. I'm J.J.
Father: What?
FLYER: J.J.!!
Father: (getting tense) What

do you mean *J.J.*!?

FLYER: My name's J.J. My friends call me J.J.

Father: Listen to me, young lady, your name is Jennifer. I'm not one of your school friends who...

FLYER: (sweetly) Sorry, but why are you calling me so early?

Father: So early? Jennifer, it's two o'clock in the afternoon!

FLYER: Tell me about it. And I'm on winter vacation.

Father: Even if school *is* on break, do you have to sleep so late?

FLYER: I'm hanging up. I'll see you when you get home from work.

Father: Wait!

FLYER: Yeah?

Father: Don't talk to me like that.

FLYER: Sorry.

Father: You don't *sound* very sorry. Young lady, you are getting to be much too...

FLYER: Why are you calling me? Don't you have work to do at that job of yours?

Father: I was calling because I think I left the stove on when I left this morning. And your mother left for work before me. I really think I forgot to turn it off.

FLYER: (calmly) Oh, I *thought* I was smelling gas fumes.

Father: (excitedly) Oh my god, Jennifer!!

FLYER: What's wrong?

Father: The gas—you'll die, the house will explode! Everything will burn down.

FLYER: What, over a few gas fumes?

Father: Jennifer! Get out of the house—open a window! Go down to the kitchen and...

FLYER: Calm down father. We don't have a gas stove. It's electric.

Father: What?

FLYER: The stove is electric—just like the heat.

Father: (more excited) No, Jennifer, the stove is gas!

FLYER: It's electric.

Father: It's gas—go turn it off.

FLYER: It's electric.

Father: Listen, I know it's gas—I cook on it. *I* pay the bills! I know the kitchen stove is gas—not electric.

FLYER: I think you're wrong.

Father: (exasperated) Don't

do this to me Jennifer. I know you don't care what happens, but I do. You could die in there. Please go down and turn off the stove.

FLYER: I'm going back to sleep. Don't worry. It'll all work out.

Father: All work out? Play it safe for once. Why can't you just go down and turn off the stove? Gas fumes are dangerous, Jennifer!

FLYER: My name's J.J.

FLYER hangs up phone, turns away from the afternoon sun and pulls blanket over her head, 99% sure that the kitchen stove is electric—*not* gas.

A FLYERS Postcard

As one would expect, FLYERS have different ways of communicating with different people. To illustrate this point, read the two versions of a postcard sent by one Robert Lewis to his young friend and to his parents, respectively.

FLYERS postcard When Sent to a Friend

HEY BO —
Florida's GR-R-E-E-A-A-T!
Girls are HOT, HOT, HOT!
How's life? Beach is a BLAST!
+ Spring Break's on a R-R-OLL!
Blowed off a bundle on New
Carrera Shades
All night Partying — MUCHO
                    Later — Rob

FLYERS Postcard When Sent to Parents

Dear mother and Father,
    Florida is a truly wonderful state.
The people are friendly. Hope all is
well. Museums and Gardens are
breathtaking. I really needed the rest.
+ sheepishly gave ½ of my money to
some poor children on beach. Can't
wait until school starts.
            Best Wishes,
                Robert

24

Staying Young
by Turning Yourself into a Trend
(or The Jane Fonda Phenomenon)

From Hollywood Child to Vassar Student, to Vietnam Opponent, to Hollywood Actress, to Political Activist, to Happy Housewife, to Diet-n-Exercise Folk Hero...

26

FLYERS' Heroes

JANE FONDA (She's a trend all by herself.)

CLINT EASTWOOD (Clint, you "make my day.")

EDDIE MURPHY (The funniest FLYER around, even if he does offend every group.)

RONALD REAGAN (FLYERS love his confidence and many love his politics.)

NANCY REAGAN (She's even better dressed than Prince and Madonna.)

TINA TURNER (The comeback queen of music—but where does she get those wild hairstyles?)

MICHAEL JACKSON (He's a thriller even if Tina Turner does have a deeper voice than he does.)

DICK CLARK (Still looks like a teenager at 55.)

LEE IACOCCA (Chrysler chairman who has proven that even business men can become celebrities.)

JULIUS ERVING (He enjoys the prestige of being called "Dr." without having to suffer through med school.)

TED TURNER (Anyone who owns his own TV network is automatically a FLYERS favorite.)

STEVEN SPIELBERG (He produces almost as many trendy movies as FLYERS watch.)

SALLY FIELD (Anyone who can play Gidget and The Flying Nun *and* become an Oscar-winning actress has the versatility that FLYERS love.)

JOE MONTANA (Male FLYERS admire this Superbowl-winning quarterback so much he could even do Pepsi commercials.)

GERALDINE FERRARO (Even if she ran for the White House with a loser, female FLYERS were inspired by Gerry.)

HARRISON FORD (An adventure series all by himself.)

ALEXIS and BLAKE CARRINGTON (So what if they're just characters on "Dynasty"—they have FLYERS style.)

CLARA "Where's the beef?" PELLER (She's over 65 but FLYERS think her commercials are more hilarious than many TV sitcoms.)

JOANNA CARSON (Anyone who can't scrape by on $35,000 a *month* in alimony must be having an amazing time.)

27

FLYERS' Favorite Losers

CHARLENE TILTON (She has a quintessential kind of body—unfortunately, it's just the kind that female FLYERS wouldn't want to have.)

ROB LOWE (Of course, FLYERS are concerned about how good they look, but Rob's probably never more than a few yards from a full-length mirror.)

KRISTY McNICHOL (Her career peaked before she hit age 18, long before most FLYERS even begin thinking about employment.)

THE BEEGEES (FLYERS know that grown men's voices just shouldn't be that high.)

DEBBIE BOONE (Barely as exciting as her father, Pat Boone.)

WALTER MONDALE (FLYERS love winners, so if you have to ask why he's on this list, where have you been since 1984?)

JULIO IGLESIAS (FLYERS think excessively sappy, romantic songs are boring.)

LISA "The Preppy Handbook" BIRNBACH (Responsible for a momentary preference toward the ridiculous nicknames Bif and Muffy.)

JULIAN LENNON (No, he doesn't want to sound just like his famous father John, does he?)

DONNY OSMOND (He probably finds milk commercials exciting.)

28

Popular FLYERS Terms and Phrases

MOST OFTEN USED MEANINGLESS PHRASES

it's like—phrase, no meaning (an easy way to ease into any sentence).

ya know—phrase, no meaning (used to fill a pause at the end of any statement).

I mean—phrase, same as "it's like."

WORDS FLYERS USE TO DESCRIBE THEMSELVES OR FAVORED EVENTS

BFOC—acronym, "Big FLYERS on Campus" (the "in" group of people).

beeper—n., one of the Beautiful People (BP).

bodacious—adj., used by male FLYERS to describe females with massive chests.

Cool biz—phrase, "That's a terrific idea!" said with an accent on the word *biz*.

FLYERS—acronym, "Fun Loving Youth En Route to Success" of course.

fresh—adj., trendy (esp. clothes, songs, etc.).

Greek—n., member of a sorority or fraternity.

hellacious—adj., wild, incredibly crazy (often applied to parties).

hunky—adj., used by female FLYERS to describe well-built males (e.g., the stars of "Miami Vice").

intense—adj., fantastic, extremely hellacious.

joint—n., the place to be. As in "This is the joint."

orgasmic—adj., exceptionally good (often used to describe foods like ice cream).

party bus—n., joint of a wild FLYERS bash. As in "Hop onto the party bus."

scene—n., same as *joint*.

scoping—v., looking for FLYERS of the opposite sex, especially while on the party bus.

totally awesome—adj., fantastic (but used in a mocking imitation of Val Speak, substitute for *tubular*).

WORDS FLYERS USE TO DESCRIBE PEOPLE AND PLACES TO BE AVOIDED

beat—adj., awful, in bad shape, to be avoided.

clueless—adj., unaware of what's going on in the FLYERS scene (i.e., anyone who hasn't heard of Prince, Cyndi Lauper, or Eddie Murphy).

copeless—adj., unable to cope with the FLYERS lifestyle.

crunchy—adj., into granola and earth tones, often used to describe art history majors. The shortened form of *crunchy-chewy* or *earthy-crunchy*.

ding—v., to be rejected (especially by a potential employer).

dweeb—n., a social reject (usually used by female FLYERS talking about males).

geek—n., incredibly hardworking student, never hops onto the party bus.

hurts, hurting—adj., same as *beat*. As in "That guy is hurting."

nerdpost—n., same as *geek*, elaboration of overused word *nerd*.

pre-————n., a derogatory prefix for someone who thinks too much about tomorrow and not enough about enjoying today. It's possible to be pre-med, pre-law, pre-professional without acting "pre-———."

pre-yuppie—n., ultimate "pre-" insult, a social and pre-professional dweeb.

social donut—n., a dweeb.

throat—n., a nerdpost.

tool—n., a throat; v., to work like a geek.

---

14 COMMON TERMS TO DESCRIBE GETTING DRUNK

bent	destroyed	torn
blitzed	ripped	trashed
bombed	rocked	twisted
deformed	shit-faced	wasted
demented	smashed	

Social Life

29

The Thursday-to-Monday FLYERS Weekend

Some might claim that college FLYERS are a wasteful group, but in reality, you won't find a more resourceful gang of young people when it comes to getting all those necessary chores done while still taking full advantage of that oh-so-important social schedule. Here's a checklist that most college FLYERS use to manage their chores while also managing their social responsibilities:

Thursday
morning Sort dirty clothes, pack them in secure box and mail home for washing.

afternoon Take inventory of munchies and party drinks. Contact liquor store and arrange for early evening delivery.

evening Eliminate "early weekend guilt" by passing through the library en route to the all-night dance club.

Friday
morning If you were foolish enough to schedule classes on a Friday, ask a friend to take good notes, then go back to sleep.

afternoon Wake up in time to catch the Friday "cliffhanger" on "All My Children."

evening   Catch up on your sleep by taking an hour nap before the 5 o'clock happy hour, the 8 o'clock movie, and the 11 o'clock party.

Saturday

morning   Try to get to sleep by 5 A.M.

afternoon   Sleep.

evening   If you're up in time, go for a jog in the afternoon sun. Otherwise, join your friends at the TV set with "Saturday Night Live" and then some late-night drinking games at the pub or local bar.

Sunday

morning   Sleep extra late.

afternoon   Read Sunday comics and take aspirin for hangover.

evening   Catch up on last week's schoolwork by photocopying a class-mate's notes.

Monday

morning   Catch up on your sleep by missing 9 o'clock class.

afternoon   Pick up clean clothes from post office.

30

Favorite Places
to Arrange Informal Get-Togethers
and Other Social Events

1. A Video Arcade
2. A McDonald's or Burger King on a Sunday Afternoon
3. Any Popular Dance Club
4. A Rock Concert
5. The Ticket Line of a Rock Concert
6. A Bowling Alley Restaurant (the sound of falling pins substitutes for background music)
7. A 24-Hour Diner Which Features Rude Busboys and Chain-Smoking Waitresses
8. The Mall (the quintessential meeting ground for FLYERS who like to shop and eat, or who like to be seen shopping and eating)
9. The Quadraplex Movie Theater. (every suburb has one)
10. Any Violent Sporting Event
11. The Reserve Room of Any College Library
12. A High School Parking Lot (on weekends only)

How FLYERS Pick Their Friends

FLYERS love to be liked. Of course they prefer the company of fellow FLYERS, but with their easy-going natures, they can easily get along with preppies, j.a.p.s, or sometimes even with yuppies (the FLYERS' extra-fun attitude compensates for the yuppie lack of personality). But FLYERS would just not want to be friends with anyone who:

• Eats pizza with a knife and fork

• Carries a calculator, ruler or spare pencils in their shirt pocket

• Organizes or joins Barry Manilow fan clubs

• Keeps an "IN" and an "OUT" basket on their desk at home

• Wants to be first on line at a Robby Benson or Kristy McNichol movie

• Finds fun in collecting blueprints to the "Star Trek" *Enterprise*

• Thinks a wild Saturday night includes a candle-

light dinner with Mom and Dad, followed by reruns of "Donny & Marie"
- Divides the day into 15-minute time blocks so he doesn't waste time on any non essential activities like his social life
- Tells people she's expecting a new lint brush for her next birthday
- Puts his name on the L.L. Bean catalog mailing list
- At a 50-keg party, insists on talking about work, the latest international disaster, or recent developments in marine biology
- Can't wait to become a yuppie

Instead, FLYERS pick their friends by looking for people who:

- Have earned a reputation for playing the most hellacious pranks on teachers or bosses
- Subscribe to *Sports Illustrated, Glamour,* or *People*
- Are credited with setting some record in bubble-blowing, Frisbee, or partying·
- Are popular enough to attract other good-looking and fun-loving friends
- Live a life that most parents would label as "unstable"

32

The 20-Point Rate-a-Party Checklist

Have you ever gotten to a party and hung around for an hour just trying to decide if you should stay for another hour—foolishly hoping the excitement would soon pick up and make your time worthwhile? Well, wait no more. With the 20-Point Rate-a-Party Checklist, you can rate a party's "fun" potential in less than ten minutes—starting as early as one week before the big event takes place.

If the party in question scores under 20 points on the checklist below, stay home and rearrange your shampoo bottles.

- If people are talking about the party 2 days in advance, add 3 points.
- If people are talking about the party 8 days in advance, add 9 points.
- If the host is your class president, add 4 points.
- If the host is the ombudsman for the Chemistry Club, subtract 6 points.
- If the party is co-sponsored by the PTA or alumni of-

fice, subtract 10 points.
- If the host asks you to bring an extra accordion, subtract 9 points.
- If Madonna or Prince are coming, add 9 points.
- If Madonna or Prince were specifically asked *not* to come, add 13 points.
- If the party is advertised as "8 until midnight," subtract 4 points.
- If the party is advertised as "11 until...," add 7 points.
- If your parents are also on the guest list, subtract 15 points.
- If the local police chief, college dean, principal, mayor, or any other government official has issued public warnings about the party, add 17 points.
- If the event is being covered by *Rolling Stone* magazine, add 10 points.
- If the event is being covered by *Readers Digest*, subtract 15 points.

33

Know Your Beers

Just as YUPPIES can distinguish Tanqueray from Gordon's in their gin and tonics, FLYERS excel in their ability to distinguish brands of beer. Although most in the over-30 crowd couldn't even tell Bud from Schmidts (some FLYERS can tell just by looking at the beer's head), FLYERS are brew experts and rate them based on 4 demanding criteria:

CHUGABILITY: If the beer doesn't have a smooth taste, you'll gag and spit it out during chugging contests.

FOAMALITY: Foam is fun. A good beer has a good head. (It's hysterical to blow foam off your brew at other people.)

BREW APPEAL: FLYERS appreciate good advertisements. The more outrageous and appealing the ads, the more popular the beer.

BURPABILITY: A crucial distinguishing factor. More burps per can mean more jokes and more fun.

Favorite Brews

BUDWEISER—The beer of choice for FLYERS. Easy to chug and more burps per can than any other.

MICHELOB—When FLYERS are buying beer with someone else's money (especially Mom and Dad's). Too expensive to chug.

ANY DARK BEER—Shows you are a real beer connoisseur and gets you out of a Bud rut. The brown foam is wild but it's tough to chug.

MOLSON and HEINEKEN —Both add an air of sophistication to an otherwise wild party.

BUD LITE and MILLER LITE —For female FLYERS who want to watch their weight or who want an easier chug. Avoided at all costs by male FLYERS.

Up & Coming Beers

MILLER—FLYERS are beginning to return to "Miller Time." High marks for burpability.

STROHS—Their wacky TV commercials are super.

SCHAEFFER—This beer's new taste is challenging Bud as the most chuggable.

ST. PAULI GIRL—Their ad ("You never forget your first girl") is the perfect cue for male FLYERS to make crude puns and tell dirty jokes. Avoided by female FLYERS.

Not for FLYERS

LOWENBRAU—Their ad ("Here's to good friends") is too sappy.

OTHER LITE BEERS— FLYERS' experienced beer palates can't take the watered-down taste. Images of chubby, middle-aged beer drinkers.

SCHMIDTS—Only ordered on a bet.

34

How FLYERS
Spend Their Vacations

It probably comes as no surprise to hear that the three most important dates on all FLYERS' calendars are the opening days of Summer Vacation, Spring Break and Winter Vacation. While the rest of the world is required to squeeze all their leisure activities into a two-week summer vacation, these Fun Loving Youths are allowed to spend more than four months of each year doing absolutely nothing.

Besides such official time off as Summer Vacation which is always three months, Winter Break which is always three weeks, and Spring Break which is always one week, there are free periods like "*mid*-winter break", "mid-term break",

"intersession", President's holidays, religious holidays, Election Day, Thanksgiving Break, Veteran's Day, and the list goes on. If you added up all these official and unofficial excuses for not going to school, you wouldn't be surprised to find that FLYERS find it hard to adjust to a 50-week-a-year work schedule when they finally enter the real world.

It's hard to plan interesting, diversified vacations. FLYERS don't lounge around aimlessly during vacation periods. Because they know how precious life really is, they busily use every minute to its fullest.

Here is how sophomores Sunny and Beepo made the most of their three vacations:

Sunny and Beepo on Spring Break

—Sunny calls TWA to make reservations for Friday morning flight to Ft. Lauderdale

—Beepo calls Ft. Lauderdale Hilton Inn to reserve a double for 6 days and 7 nights

—Sunny and Beepo go to bank and withdraw $250 each from their parents' accounts for spending money

—Sunny picks up two new bikinis she saw advertised in *Glamour*

—Beepo and Sunny skip Friday classes and arrive in Florida just in time for Student's Happy Hour at a jazz club near the hotel

—Beepo and Sunny spend the next 6 days on the beach partaking in such activities as surfing, suntanning, volleyball and beach party cookouts

—Beepo and Sunny return to school 7 days later, exhausted and in need of another week's vacation before going back to class.

Sunny and Beepo on Winter Vacation

—Sunny calls Delta to make reservations for Friday morning flight to Honolulu

—Beepo calls Hyatt Regency Waikiki to reserve a double for 6 days and 7 nights

—Beepo and Sunny go to bank and withdraw $250 each from their parents' accounts for spending money

—Sunny picks up two new bikinis she saw advertised in *Cosmopolitan*

—Beepo and Sunny skip Friday classes and arrive in Hawaii just in time for Student's Happy Hour at a rock club near the hotel

—Beepo and Sunny spend the next 6 days on the beach partaking in such activities as surfing, suntanning, volleyball and beach party cookouts

—Beepo and Sunny return to school 7 days later, exhausted and in need of another week's vacation before going back to class.

Sunny and Beepo on Summer Vacation

—Sunny calls People's Express to make reservations for Friday flight to London with connecting flight to Nice, France

—Beepo calls Hyatt-Regency in Nice to reserve a double for 6 days and 7 nights

—Beepo and Sunny go to bank and withdraw $500 each from their parents' accounts for spending money

—Sunny picks up two new bikinis she saw advertised in *Mademoiselle*

—Beepo and Sunny miss the last day of their summer jobs and arrive in France just in time for Student's Happy Hour at a bistro near the hotel

—Beepo and Sunny spend the next 6 days on the beach partaking in such activities as surfing, suntanning, volleyball and beach party cookouts

—Beepo and Sunny return home, exhausted and in need of American home-cooking before going back to school.

35

The Right and Wrong Sports

FLYERS enjoy both playing and watching sports. In addition to the traditional foot-hockey, and soccer, here is a list of right and wrong sports for FLYERS:

To Do	*Don't Even Watch*
Water Skiing	**Figure Skating (for men)**
Volleyball (only on the beach)	**Archery**
	Badminton
Frisbee	**Rugby (for women)**
Windsurfing	**Bird Watching**
Skydiving	**Horseshoes**
Roller Skating	**Miniature Golf**
Pool	**Synchronized Swimming**
Skiing	**Fencing**
Ping-Pong	**Croquet (if taken seriously)**
Racquetball	
Skateboarding	**Crew/Rowing (too painful for the fun loving)**
Croquet (if played in wacky costume)	
Stickball	
Surfing	
Ice Skating	
Lacrosse	
Street Hockey	
White-Water Rafting	
Tennis	
Mountain Climbing	
Professional Wrestling (to watch, only as long as you don't believe it's real)	

The Wrong Sport   The Right Sport

36

Favorite Games

Games are an important part of FLYERS' lives—they break up the endless monotony of going to movies, concerts, and parties. Here are the favorite games of this fun loving group:

FRISBEE—Tossing this round piece of plastic has come to represent FLYERS' relaxed, outdoorsy style. Being able to throw and catch backhand and under the legs are essential FLYERS' skills. FLYERS' dogs have to be able to play frisbee too.

VIDEO GAMES—As much fun as you can possibly have for a quarter. The video arcade is also a great place for female FLYERS to pick up guys, since the ratio is usually in their favor.

TRIVIAL PURSUIT—Usually played with teams.

FLYERS excel in sports and leisure questions (areas where they have a lot of personal experience). History questions are avoided since keeping track of what happened last week is tough enough.

POKER—Gives FLYERS an excuse to drink beer even though they're not playing a drinking game.

HACKY SAC—Nowadays almost anyone can throw a frisbee, but only FLYERS can keep this little bean bag aloft using only their feet.

DRINKING GAMES:

QUARTERS—The quintessential FLYERS drinking game. Players try to bounce a .quarter off a table into a small glass of beer. If you're successful, you point with your elbow (a strictly enforced game rule) at whoever you want to take a drink. That person chugs the beer, catching the quarter in his/her teeth. Good natured revenge on anyone who hits you to drink is the hallmark of this popular game.

"HI BOB"—Played while watching reruns of the old "Bob Newhart Show." Players pass around a glass of beer and whoever is holding the glass when a character says, "Hi Bob" (in some half-hour shows it happens up to 20 times) drinks the beer. Strategy is extremely important, since you can hold the glass for as long as you want.

SOAP OPERA SIP—A relaxed drinking game used in order to warm up for Happy Hour, played while watching "All My Children" or "General Hospital." Each player picks their favorite character on the soap. Every time that character speaks, you take a sip of beer. The game really gets moving with each fast-paced argument on the show.

Key Lines to Use
and *Not* to Use When Flirting
in the Laundry Room
or Local Dance Club

At the Supermarket

Use: "Hello Beautiful—Wanna go out to the parking lot and see the backseat of my Porsche upside down?"

Don't use: "Hello Handsome—They're having a sale on deodorant over in aisle four—thought you'd want to know."

"Hello Beautiful—I can show you where to find a bigger banana."

At the Laundry Room

Use: "Hello Handsome—If you run out of change, you're welcome to mix your clothes with mine. I've got anti-static Borax."

Don't use: "Hello Beautiful—Do they really make bras that small?"

"Hello Handsome—That's the tiniest jockstrap I've ever seen in my whole life. Is it real?"

At the Club

Use:	"Hello Handsome—I guess you finally realized I am the most desirable girl in this whole pathetic room."
Don't use:	"Hello Beautiful—Did anyone ever tell you that you've got Phyllis Diller's eyes?" "Hello Handsome—I got double 800's on my SAT's—wanna dance?"

At the Tennis Court

Use:	"Hello Handsome—I'll bet you've gotta have a steady muscle to guide one of those heavy magnesium rackets."
Don't use:	"Hello Beautiful—Do you want to play with my balls?" "Hello Handsome—What would you do if I let you beat me?"

38

How FLYERS Look at "Falling in Love"

Lately, we've heard a lot about yuppies in love and preppies in love. What about FLYERS in love? Here's how FLYERS react when they've been hit by Cupid's arrow.

—FLYERS IN LOVE DO:

- walk with their hands in each other's back pockets
- start to identify with soap opera characters like Erica of "All My Children" and Luke of "General Hospital"
- avoid talking about "commitment" until they've hit age 30
- make love whenever they feel the urge to shock friends, roommates, relatives or strangers
- call "Dr. Ruth's" radio show and disguise their voices
- talk about sex more often than they talk about school, work, money, music, cars or food

—FLYERS IN LOVE DON'T:

- write romantic poetry
- record Linda Ronstadt's love songs for old-time's sake
- cheat on each other—if there's any possibility that they might be caught
- threaten to drink poison when a relationship is all over
- hide their affection in public
- send "strip-a-grams" to each other, unless they can blame the stunt on someone else

A Typical Romantic Conversation
Between Two FLYERS
on Their First Date

A sporty convertible being driven by a 20-year-old male stops at a street corner. A brunette with tight blue jeans and a long shoulder bag walks up to the car and puts her hands on her hips.

DeDe: It's about time you got here. These new Candies are killing my feet!

Dex: I'm not late.

DeDe: Not a bad car.

Dex: Get in.

DeDe: And vinyl seats too— how plush!

Dex: Turn the stereo on. That's a 3004 Blaupunkt —I put it in myself.

DeDe: What time is it? My Swatch ran down. Can you believe? And you know, it cost a fortune.

Dex: Where d'ya wanna go?

DeDe: You like my 501's? They were marked *up* to $38.50.

Dex: How 'bout Mickey D's?

DeDe: M.J.'s birthday is tomorrow. Another expense for me to bear—or at least for my *parents* to bear.

Dex: They finally start putting milk in those shakes— and you talk about thick. *Wickedly* thick!

DeDe: Well I'm getting her the cutest little swimsuit. It's a Speedo.

Dex: We used to get burgers

at Tasty Fingers until they found that toasted rat in the six-piece Big Bucket Surprise. To think we used to wolf down a whole bucket in five minutes.

DeDe: I looked at the Jantzen's and ran over to J.C. Penney, but I just decided M.J. isn't worth all that trouble. Speedos are good enough.

Dex: And they started playing the worst music in the parking lot too. We're talking Lawrence Welk and crap like they play in supermarkets.

DeDe: Ready for midterms?

Dex: And they had the worst pizza—like cardboard. Made Pizza Hut taste like French cuisine.

DeDe: Well I'm sure we'll all do well on them—I'm counting on *Monarch Notes* to pull me through English Lit.

Dex: Gimme three bucks for the gas. My mom took back the Exxon card.

DeDe: My dad's getting me a summer job in his office. How 'bout that?

Dex: Change that station, huh? Use the electronic signal search button. Ever seen one like that?

DeDe: M.J.'s gonna be lifeguarding again, can ya believe? The girl can't even swim. I feel sorry for the poor soul who decides to drown while *she's* on duty.

Dex: Bought some tickets to see the 49'ers. Thirty bucks a shot.

DeDe: So Dan—tell me more about yourself. M.J. said you...

Dex: Dex.

DeDe: Dex? I thought you went by "Dan."

Dex: Why would I go by "Dan"?

DeDe: I thought your name was Dan Bookbinder. Aren't you the blind date Mary Jo Roperman set up for me?

Dex: No! Do I look like a blind date? I'm Poindexter Peterson—Gigi Peterson's brother!

DeDe: Who?

Dex: Peterson! Who the hell are *you*?!

DeDe: I'm Dolores Smithers—who'd ya think I was?

Dex: You're supposed to be an ugly friend of my sister's, and I'm supposed to be doing her a big favor by taking you to dinner.

DeDe: Big favor? Ugly friend? *I* was supposed to be picked up on the corner of Elm and Grove Street in a metallic white Ford Mustang convertible by a blind date whose name was Dan—Dan Bookbinder, I thought.

Dex: Well this happens to be a metallic ivory Mercury Cougar convertible, and *my* name's Dex Peterson.

DeDe: Is this some stupid joke? Let me out of this car! Stop at the curb you moron!

Dex: Sure sweetheart. Thanks a lot for burning up my gasoline!

DeDe: Yeah creep—and thanks for screwing up my evening!

Campus Lifestyle

40

How FLYERS
Pick Their Colleges

FLYERS maintain certain standards when selecting the appropriate college. It's an important step in their lives, and it must be carried out properly. Here are some of the rules to keep in mind if you want to follow the FLYERS method of choosing a college:

—Never choose a school that puts you within "dropping in" distance of your home. Parents will think twice about surprising you on a Sunday morning if they know the drive will take five hours.

—Make sure the athletic budget of the university is not exceeded by the amount spent on biological research.

—Never apply to a college whose catalog advertises, "Many of our students like to cook their own meals after freshman year." All

this means is that the dining hall food stinks.

—Avoid schools located in states with a drinking age higher than 19.

—Try to look for colleges with at least 6000 students. Anonymity is important.

—For Women especially: Single-sex schools can be the kiss of death if there are no co-ed colleges or major sources of social life nearby.

—Unless you have the same security concerns as a Saudi prince or Brooke Shields, avoid schools that have curfews, dorm mothers, or night-time room checks.

—If the school housing office has a rule against popcorn poppers, electric blankets or deep-dish doughnut friers, choose another college. It's not worth sacrificing your comfort.

THE FLYERS' FAVORITE COLLEGES
"The Top 25"

1. **Boston University** (Boston, Mass.)—Close to the water and close to the best dance clubs in New England.
2. **Case Western Reserve** (Cleveland, Ohio)—If you have to be in Ohio, Cleveland is the only city with a nightlife.
3. **Duke University** (Durham, North Carolina)—Perfect Frisbee campus.
4. **Emory University** (Atlanta, Georgia)— Since this is a Coca-Cola city, FLYERS have good reason to like this school.
5. **Georgetown University** (Washington, D.C.)—The shops, the bars, and all the students make the politics seem nonexistent.
6. **New York University** (New York, New York)—Great clubs, wild people, the Village, etc.
7. **Northwestern University** (Chicago, Illinois)   —Since the University of Chicago is too hardcore, this is the logical choice.
8. **Ohio State** (Columbus, Ohio)—Constant partying and great football.
9. **Penn State** (University Park, Pennsylvania)—Ditto.
10. **Southern Methodist University** (Dallas, Texas)—J.R.   Ewing went here.
11. **UCLA** (Los Angeles, California)—Because it's in California—and that's reason enough.
12. **U.C. Berkeley** (Berkeley, San Francisco, California)—Their reputation from the 1960s attracts FLYERS.
13. **University of Colorado** (Boulder, Colorado)—Mucho partying and skiing.
14. **University of Georgia** (Athens, Georgia)—Some of the best frats in the country.

15. **University of Hawaii** (Honolulu, Hawaii)—TV show "Hawaii Five-O" gave this state universal appeal.
16. **University of Massachussetts** (Amherst, Massachusetts)—They nicknamed this place "Zoo Mass."
17. **University of Maryland** (College Park, Maryland)—If you're looking for anonymity, yet still want to be near friendly people, this is the place.
18. **University of Miami** (Coral Gables, Florida)—Spring break can last throughout the year.
19. **University of Minnesota** (Minneapolis, Minnesota)—One of only a few reasons to spend four years in sub-zero weather.
20. **University of Wisconsin** (Madison, Wisconsin)—The only college that is bigger than your hometown.
21. **University of North Carolina** (Chapel Hill, North Carolina)—Great frats, but don't be fooled—these people work hard.
22. **University of Southern California** (Los Angeles, California)—A glorious year-round tanning center with smart Californians. What could be better?
23. **University of Texas** (Austin, Texas)—Lots of oil money here. Learn how to spend money like the Texans.
24. **Notre Dame** (Notre Dame, Indiana)—Knute Rockne gave this school's football team historical significance.
25. **University of Florida** (Gainesville, Florida)—Although it's a good school, your parents will swear you're hanging out at the beach.

"The Runners-Up"

1. **Kansas State University** (Manhattan, Kansas)
2. **Louisiana State University** (Baton Rouge, Louisiana)

3. **Purdue University** (Lafayette, Indiana)
4. **Syracuse University** (Syracuse, New York)
5. **University of Michigan** (Ann Arbor, Michigan)
6. **University of Houston** (Houston, Texas)
7. **Temple University** (Philadelphia, Pennsylvania)

"For Ivy League FLYERS"

1. **Harvard** —It's big, it's in Boston, and it's inspired a whole shopping area called Cambridge and Harvard Square.
2. **Princeton** —In spite of the workload and the preppies, the few celebrities and children of royalty manage to make the place exciting.
3. **Yale** —Jennifer *Flashdance* Beals made this New Haven school acceptable for FLYERS.
4. **Dartmouth** —Almost too far from the civilized world. But saved by the frats.
5. **Columbia** —Almost too close to the uncivilized world. But saved by the dance clubs.
6. **Brown** —Trendiest of the Ivies. Needs no celebrities to give it FLYERS status.
7. **Cornell** —Good choice, if just for the sororities and frats. It gets so cold here, skipping class during the winter is justified.
8. **University of Pennsylvania** —New clothes and charge cards, yet non-Easterners confuse it with Penn State.

Schools That FLYERS Avoid

1. **MIT (and if you forget what that stands for, Massachussetts Institute of Technology)**
2. **CIT (yeah, California's got one of these too)**
3. **Oral Roberts University**
4. **Convent of the Sacred Heart (or anything that sounds like it)**
5. **RPI (Rensselaer Polytechnic Institute)**

41

Decorating a FLYERS Dorm Room

Tidy and orderly are two words never used to describe a FLYERS dorm room. See if you can meet the challenge of finding all 40 of the following items in the sketch of a typical room (a few hints are provided):

1. Nerf basketball hoop (on wall over garbage can)
2. Overflowing garbage can
3. Dirty laundry (in pile on floor)
4. School books (under dirty laundry)
5. Basketball
6. Broken hockey stick

Bookcase on which can be found:
7. No books (see #4)
8. Beer can collection
9. Stack of pots and dishes (brought from home but never used)
10. Liquor bottles: Jack Daniels, cheap gin, cheap vodka
11. Stock of Fritos, Cheetos, and Doritos
12. Record/tape collection
13. Stereo
14. One humungous stereo speaker
15. Other tremendous speaker (by window to blast music outside)
16. Dirty sweats and towel (on top of speaker #15)
17. One ski (don't ask what happened to the other one)
18. Skateboard (one missing wheel)
19. Desk (rarely used but well cluttered)
20. Touch-tone phone (under desk clutter)
21. Desk lamp (no light bulb)
22. Frame with picture of latest love (changed biweekly)
23. Dust balls

Posters on wall:

24. Movie star hunk/*Sports Illustrated* poster girl
25. Favorite musical group
26. Favorite product (e.g. beer)
27. Bandanna (covering sole lightbulb in room)

28. Small free weights
29. Frisbee
30. 12-inch portable TV (gym shorts hanging from antenna)
31. Digital clock radio (17 minutes fast to prevent missing important appointments—FLYERS think its 8 minutes slow)
32. Unmade bed (clump of linen service sheets and blanket)
33. *People* and *Rolling Stone* (on bed)
34. Funny hat and Hawaiian lei (from last week's theme parties)
35. One Adidas, one Nike, one Tretorn

Closet filled with:
36. Full laundry bag (to be mailed home)

37. Sweatshirts and T-shirts (crumpled on shelf)
38. Jeans and Cut-off cords (on hangers)
39. Cardboard Michelob six-bottle holder (used to carry soap and shampoo to shower)
40. Popcorn popper and hot pot (hidden under T-shirts—violates college housing rules)

Not found:
- Hot tub or Jacuzzi (couldn't fit through door)
- Telephone answering machine (too pre-professional)

42

The Campus:
Why FLYERS Congregate
Around Schools When
They Never Go to Class

Of course, not all FLYERS go or have gone to college. Some have a crazy idea that in order to go to college you must either like homework or enjoy pulling "all-nighters" to pass a test. (A major public relations effort by college administrators and parents has caused many to actually believe these outrageous lies.) In order to dispel the falsehoods about college life, the *real* reasons why all FLYERS should demand to go away to college are listed below:

1. Gives your parents a reason to buy you a new car and stereo (or at least you

might have a chance of convincing them to do so).

2. Have 35 more hours each week to party. (Explanation: In high school, you had about 35 hours of school each week—all required. In college, you may have 18 hours of classes but attendance is rarely if ever taken—so they're not really required at all. This frees up 35 more hours for your important social life.)

3. Develop those enjoyable bad habits your parents would try to break you of if you were around the house.

4. Meet other FLYERS, especially those of the opposite sex.

5. Break minor laws and get away with it (by claiming you were involved in a sorority or fraternity initiation prank).

6. You can explain to your parents that you're always so exhausted because of late nights spent in the library. (They'll never need to know about those four-day party weekends, and there's no reason to worry them about it.)

7. You never have to make your bed or clean your room.

8. Get parents to pay for winter and spring vacations so you can relax from all the schoolwork you claim to have done (but haven't).

9. The awful cafeteria food gives you an excuse to eat fast food and junk food.

10. Parties can last longer and be wilder on college campuses—away from the rest of civilized society.

11. Make your parents think you're making good use of your time (going to movies, watching TV, and playing frisbee is good use of time).

12. Learn obscure facts which you'll never have to remember after the final. When do you think was the last time Bill Cosby (Ph.D., University of Massachusetts) was asked about the causes of the War of 1812, or Ronald Reagan (B.A., Eureka College) was asked about the themes in *Moby Dick*?

13. Develop b.s. into a fine art through numerous social science and English courses. This is an essential skill for anyone planning for a successful future in any high-paying but extremely easy job.

14. Your parents can't impose a curfew, regardless of what you do wrong.

15. Have an excuse to buy more sweatshirts and T-shirts (all of course with your college's insignia).

16. Gives your parents the opportunity to put a school decal in the back window of their car.

17. Improve your fun loving image. No one at college needs to know that you only had one date during high school, or about how you lost the championship game.

18. Avoid choosing a career for at least four more years— even longer if you go to grad school.

Picking Your Roommate and the 4 Types FLYERS Try to Avoid

Before you make the awful mistake of agreeing to room with someone just because he or she seems like a nice person, think *again*! Don't rely on your intuition when selecting a roommate. Play it safe by asking all prospects the following questions:

1. Do you have a late model Firebird or Corvette?

2. Do you enjoy performing occasional housework?
3. Do you have a good-looking, unattached brother or sister who is around our age?
4. Is your mother a good cook; is she the "dropping in" type?
5. By any chance do you wear a size-eight shoe?
6. Are you generous with your money?

7. Do you have any experience typing research papers under a tight deadline?

8. Do minor things upset you, like when others fly off the handle and break your records because of a temporary loss of mental stability?

Once you have collected the answers to these questions, you can scrutinize them carefully and end up with an ideal roommate. *Or*, you can ignore these questions and chance getting a roommate who is a *Geek*, a *Material Girl*, an *Acid Head*, or a *Jock*.

The Geek will bore you out of your mind. Generally lacking in cleanliness and social graces, the Geek will never look you in the face, even though he'll talk for hours on end about God knows what. Whether it's a math equation, a new sci-fi novel or a speck of dust sitting in the corner, the Geek will talk about a subject for so long and in such great detail that you'll be ready to

The Geek

shove his pet frog and Texas Instrument calculator down the electric Disposall. The only benefit to living with a Geek is that when you get angry and beat him up, he will always be too weak and scared to fight back.

The Material Girl will spend your money—*every* cent of it. Whether she puts pressure on you to buy expensive little things for *her*, or to buy expensive little things for *yourself*, you'll be declaring bankruptcy within months. She whines, nags and complains. Her goals? Merely to

The Material Girl

The Acid Head thinks he is too cool for words. Always in transit, you'll never catch him without car keys in hand. Besides his drugs, his only other prize possessions are his black Camaro and his dark Ray Bans, which he wears to hide his drugged-out, bloodshot eyes. If you like to have personal space you'll get it, because the Acid Head will almost never be around. Of course, his friends and customers will be calling

have the very best of everything. The Material Girl is a lot of fun when you're happy and when she's happy. But just wait until you're no longer a part of the "in" group. She'll drop you faster than a bounced check. The only redeeming quality of the Material Girl is that she usually keeps reasonable hours. Always trying to catch up on her beauty sleep, she will turn in at 10:00 P.M. and let you catch another one or two hours of sanity before she starts all over again at 8:00 A.M. the next morning.

The Acid Head

at hours ranging from 8:00 A.M. until 1:00 A.M., but that might be a small price to pay in order to keep your own room or your apartment from becoming a target for the narcotics squad. The less the Acid Head comes by, the more ignorance you can display when the cops arrive.

The Jock will do very little for your social life or peace of mind. Not only will she intentionally scare off handsome gentlemen who come knocking, but she will "accidentally" break your vanity mirror, "accidentally" drop your Tina Turner albums, and "accidentally" step on your Sony Walkman (you get the drift). The Jock pretends not to care about your busy social life, but she is actually envious of any attention paid to you by potential boy-

The Jock

friends, by milkmen, or even by telephone operators. Stay on her good side by not creasing the sports pages and by not ironing her field hockey jerseys.

44

Favorite Pranks of FLYERS

What makes FLYERS' pranks so hilarious is their originality and spontaneity. Yet, there are many tried and true pranks which are always good for a laugh:

Alka Seltzer Shower— Crush about 20 Alka Seltzer tablets and sprinkle them on the floor of the shower. When the unsuspecting target turns on the shower, his/her feet will be in for a fizzing surprise.

Psyche Out—A great stunt to pull on throats and geeks. Go with a large group of FLYERS to a well-known buster of an exam. Ten minutes into the test, the pranksters all stand up and hand in their supposedly completed papers while murmuring things like: "What a breeze. That was my easiest exam this semester." Designed to psyche out even the hardest of the hardcore nerds.

Pennying In—Simply jam some pennies into a door around its hinges. Anyone inside the room won't be able to open the door. For a really great laugh, see what the person does when you pull the fire alarm.

Foreign Student Confusion—Tell foreign students incorrect meanings of various slang terms and phrases. For example, explain that the proper greeting for a pretty woman is "What's up bitch?" and that the correct way to thank someone for helping you is "Thanks, asshole."

Watering Down—Fill several large trash cans with water and pour them under the door of the target's room. Especially humorous when done while the target has a date over for a romantic evening.

Hairless Prank—Put Nair (women's hair remover) into a guy's shorts or onto his legs while he's sleeping. Sure to cause a big surprise once he takes a look.

Mass Flush—In many dorms, when the john is flushed, the shower gets hotter. So when the target begins to take a shower, a group goes and repeatedly flushes the toilets. (Only considered a success if you can get a good scream from the target.)

Ima Pig—Major prank played on the school's administration by a large group of FLYERS (especially so-rorities and fraternities). An animal (like the school's mascot) or a fictitious person is enrolled in the school. The pranksters work together to take classes and do school-work for it. In four years, the animal or imaginary person gets a college degree, often with better grades than any of the individuals involved.

Shower Caper—Take the robe and/or towel of a guy or girl from the bathroom while they are taking a shower. Get a large group to-gether to wait at the target's door when they return with little (if anything) on. Espe-cially popular when done to members of the opposite sex.

45

Spiral vs. Looseleaf:
The Notebook Controversy

We have all faced the perennial problem of trying to decide which type of notebook is more practical—the spiral or the looseleaf. For each new course, each new job, each new assignment, we are put in the uncomfortable position of having to decide where to record important information. Well, FLYERS have learned the benefits and weaknesses of both notebook styles.

Common Sense Advantages to Using a Looseleaf Notebook

- Allows for easy release of papers when you drive out of parking lot on last day of school, littering the campus and main road with nine months of paperwork and problem sets
- Allows you to carry the paperwork for all of your courses at one time

- If lost, gives you an excuse for being unprepared in all of your courses at one time
- According to a University of Miami student, when wrapped with tin foil, an unfolded looseleaf works as a marvelous suntanning reflector

Common Sense Advantages to Using a Spiral Notebook

- Undoubtedly looks more mature than a looseleaf
- Prevents embarrassing "paper tornadoes" when school bully pushes you down the staircase and your notebook flies into the air
- More manageable for note-taking when using those "smaller-than-life-sized" desk tops in large lecture halls
- Gives the appearance that you're neat and organized even when you're not

46

A Typical FLYERS Courseload

Courses that FLYERS take (since "take" implies that one actually goes to the class with some regularity, it's probably better to say "Courses that FLYERS register in" or "Courses that FLYERS cut") can be divided into three types:

I. **The Gut or Blow-Off or Mickey Mouse**—Enjoyable and extremely easy class, with the emphasis on extremely.

II. **The Resume Padder**—Not too tough but practical. Looks good on a resume.

III. **The Buster**—Taught by an infamous and sadistic professor who longs for the good old days of corporal punishment. Also any advanced math, science or engineering course.

GUTS AND BLOW-OFFS

Although the blow-offs at each school vary, there are eight common ones (one to be taken each semester):

- **Astrogut** (Introduction to Astronomy)—Class usually includes a chance to use a telescope (and insist you spotted a UFO), and a visit to a planetarium for a laser light show.

- **Clapping for Credit** (Music Appreciation)—By covering nearly two centuries of music history each month, this course provides FLYERS with the basic information they need to seem cultured but avoids any messy details which might unnecessarily tax the FLYERS' minds.

- **Darkness at Noon** (Art Appreciation)—Similar to "Clapping for Credit," but since lectures revolve around the use of slides, the darkened classroom gives FLYERS a chance to nap after a big lunch or to sleep off that hangover from the night before.

- **Intro to Sociology** — Universally so easy that it doesn't even need a code name.

- **Learning to Talk** (Public Speaking)—FLYERS have been talking to people for a long time and deserve to get college credit for having learned such a demanding skill. Remember, very few people who can't speak have made it big.

- **Physics for Poets** (Intro Physics for Non-Science Majors)—Class which

teaches FLYERS the reason why everything that goes up must come down. Although this reason is forgotten as soon as the exam ends, FLYERS continue to remember the importance of this concept whenever they drop water balloons from their dorm room windows.

- **Rocks for Jocks** (Intro Geology)—Often includes a field trip to find rocks, and a visit to a museum.

- **Sluts and Nuts** (Intro Psychology) —Allows FLYERS to use sophisticated, clinical language to describe non-FLYERS (e.g. "He is still in the Freudian anal-retentive stage," instead of the more crude "That dork has a stick up his behind").

- **Tuesday Night at the Movies** (Film Criticism)—Bring some popcorn and beer to class and watch some great old movies.

RESUME PADDERS

These courses include introductory business, economics, and other pre-professional prep (P-cubed for those in the know) courses. These courses are necessary to balance off guts, since future employers (at least some of whom are FLYERS and know how little work a blow-off can be) want to think that FLYERS will be well qualified for their companies. Taking these courses also satifies parents who are afraid that their FLYERS children are spending thousands of dollars to attend a four-year-long party (which they actually are).

BUSTERS

FLYERS never willingly take a buster: they either have to take it in order to graduate or they do so by mistake (one hilarious FLYERS prank is to tell someone that a buster is a gut). When FLYERS do take a buster, they always do it with a group. At least they can joke about the course and the professor both inside and outside of class (using a mirror to shine a light on the professor's forehead during a boring buster lecture will earn high praise from fellow FLYERS). Taking a buster with a group also allows the work to be divided up among several people, making some buster courses even easier than some guts.

FLYERS Tip #3:
How to Get in Good
with Teachers with Little
or No Effort

Just because you want a good grade doesn't mean you have to work for it. As any Fun Loving Youth En Route to Success will tell you, there are quick and easy ways to get top grades for little or no effort. Here's how to do it when you're—

Going for the "A":

... During lunchtime, wedge soda bottles underneath your teacher's car wheels. Just before school is over, tell your teacher that you saw the three toughest kids in the school playing a dirty prank

on him and that he should take notice of soda bottles under his car. The unsuspecting teacher will think you're a real hero for telling on classmates who could surely beat your brains out.

Going for the "B":

... Even though teacher evaluations are supposed to remain anonymous, be sure to identify yourself in some manner when filling out a highly positive evaluation form. You can give your identity away by saying such things as: "When my brother Sam had Mrs. Smith just two years before me..." or "Since I sat directly in front of Mrs. Smith each Monday and Wednesday morning, I can gladly say..." These instant "give-aways" will allow your teacher to reward you for a flattering evaluation.

Going for the "C":

... Half way through the semester, visit the department chairman for each of your respective courses. Tell each of them that your respective professor is the best that you've ever had, and how everyone should know that Professor Jones (Professor Davis, Professor Smith, etc.) is a credit to the department.

The chairman will certainly tell the professor about your visit and your kind remarks. Higher grades will start to trickle in.

Going for the "D":

... FLYERS don't aim for Ds. If you're En Route to Success, a "D" won't get you there.

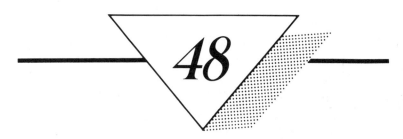

Cafeteria Etiquette

Here, Mr. Rudeness, the foremost expert on *excruciating* behavior, answers a few questions from his mailbag of letters in order to help FLYERS when they dine in the cafeteria:

Dear Mr. Rudeness,
What is the proper food with which to begin a food fight?
Mischief-maker in Massachusetts

Dear Mischief,

Small, wet and mushy foods, easily catapulted for long ranges by a spoon, are best. A good alternative is any already-chewed food spit out onto a spoon.

Dear Mr. Rudeness,

When eating mystery meat stew must I drink white milk or can I choose a chocolate milk?

Interested in Illinois

Dear I.i.I,

Chocolate milk is *de rigeur* for a meat dinner. More important, if you begin to laugh hysterically while drinking chocolate milk, it looks much better when it begins running out of your nose.

Dear Mr. Rudeness,

What are the correct utensils to use when having a cafeteria health food platter of fried pork ribs, mashed potatoes, banana split, and bean sprout salad?

Curious in California

Dear C.C.,

You need to be more adventurous. Don't use any utensils at all. Just dig your hands right into that slop. A popular custom is to use the shirt of the person sitting to your right as a napkin. Give it a try.

Dear Mr. Rudeness,

Every day a real dweeb comes to sit at our lunch table. How can I tell this wonk to sit somewhere else?

Nervous New Yorker

Dear Nervous,

Don't hurt the poor geek's feelings with harsh words. Actions speak much louder than words. I suggest the next time this nerdpost plants himself down at your exclusive table, everyone should quietly get up, walk slowly over to his seat, and simultaneously vomit all over his food tray. Repeat the process daily, until the reject gets this subtle hint.

49

Preparing the FLYERS Meal When You're Not on a Meal Plan

FLYERS are not known for their cooking ability. Why? Cooking is boring, and clean-up is done only under the threat of losing this week's allowance. More importantly, it's tough to cook and play frisbee at the same time (although it has been done). When FLYERS have no choice but to cook, they use their ingenuity and simply:

OPEN A BOX For the most important occasions. Just give it ten minutes in the microwave and your frozen TV dinner of chicken leg, mashed potatoes, and green beans is an elegant three-course meal. Surprise your lucky dinner guests with a delicious dessert—open up a box of Yodels or Captain Crunch.

OPEN A CAN Unfortunately, canned food just doesn't have that same fresh flavor of boxed food. But the variety is so much greater that it's often worth the bother of having to use a can opener.

OPEN A JAR When you want to be more casual than eating from a box or can. Peanut butter, Marshmallow Fluff, pickles, maraschino cherries and many other delicious and nutritious foods are found in jars. Perfect for an informal dinner party or buffet, when TV dinners would be too much trouble.

OPEN A BAG FLYERS know that Fritos, popcorn, potato chips, Cheetos and Doritos can make a nutritious vegetarian meal of corn, potatoes, and cheese.

OPEN A TELEPHONE BOOK Ordering out for pizza or Chinese food is essential at least twice a week, when the monotony of all this gourmet cooking gets to be too much.

Cleaning Up The Mess

- FLYERS are ingenious when it comes to "clean-up time." By using paper plates and plastic utensils, everything is disposable.
- When using real dishes, FLYERS simply leave them dirty in the sink until someone else, who really needs the plates, goes ahead and washes them.
- Another easy way to clean up real dishes: just oh-so-accidentally knock the plates off the table. Then throw out the broken pieces.

Roadtripping: Do FLYERS Really Do It and Why

Yes, the relatively all-male activity of roadtripping to single-sex schools carries on. You might wonder why FLYERS go roadtripping when there are so many co-ed colleges.

You might wonder why these guys get together each weekend, pile into a cramped car, drive for hours, spend a fortune on gas, visit women's colleges, crash their formal parties, sleep with women they hardly know, and then drive back home the next morning. You might wonder why.

Speaking to a representative sample of frequent roadtrippers, we asked the question "Why do you go roadtripping?" Here's what we were told:

Slip, a junior—"I go road-tripping because it's a great way to flirt and still avoid commitment."

Lax, a senior—"It's like a whole social experience—like a whole elevating and introspective situation. Getting drunk, sleeping with people who've got no inhibitions, totaling a rented car, getting lost on I-95 or some turnpike. It's all a part of maturing."

Boozer, a sophomore—"It's the *in* thing to do these days."

Cecil, a sophomore (this guy is a loser)—"Gee, well

none of the girls in my school are pretty enough for me."

Drill, a medical student—"It's a great way to look for a wife."

Spud, a junior—"I go because I don't feel like such a loser when I strike out with a girl. If I struck out all the time at my own school, I'd get a bad rep on campus. When a school is an hour away I know I'm safe."

No female in our survey would admit to being a road-tripper. (Understandably so, since there are only four or five all-male colleges left in the U.S.)

How Male FLYERS Should Arrange a Roadtrip

a) find a classmate who's got a sister at an all-female school within two hours' driving time
b) get a group of four or five guys and make sure one has a car, preferably a convertible
c) call the target school and make sure they won't be on vacation when you get there
d) be sure your "contact" has a good sense of humor and some good-looking friends
e) bring a notebook (as a disguise) just in case you have to scope out possibilities in the target school's library
f) when arriving at the target campus, get your friends to agree on a meeting place and meeting time—in case you get split up
g) never plan to stay more than 24 hours
h) never visit during Parents' Weekend, and avoid bringing large pieces of luggage

51

Sororities, Fraternities, and Other Social Clubs to Join

It's sometimes tough for FLYERS to decide which of several social organizations to join. But with this simple rating system, it will be a breeze to determine the best one (and also to be absolutely sure you won't join one you should avoid).

1. What type of facilities does the house have:
   Shares small house with another sorority or
   frat   +12
   Three-floor house   +34
   Three-floor house with beer on tap   +137
   55-room mansion on 12 acres with
   swimming pool   +138
   55-room mansion on 12 acres with
   swimming pool and beer on tap   +298
   Club president's 8' × 10' dorm room   AVOID

2. Grade point average of house members:
   B (3.0)   +42
   C (2.0)   +56
   Total of 2.0 for entire house   +78
   A+ or better   AVOID

3. Number of people who attended the last house party:

Less than 100	−14
101–250	+26
251–1000	+67
More than 1000	+89
19 (Madonna, Mick Jagger, Jennifer Beals, Tom Cruise and 15 club members)	+346
None (final exams are coming up in just six months)	AVOID

4. The greatest success of the house's most famous alumnus:

President of a major corporation	+30
Professional athlete	+48
Starred in major motion picture or recorded gold album	+69
Owns a McDonald's (just ten minutes from campus)	+99
Plays back-up music for Wayne Newton	AVOID

5. The first question house members ask you is:

"Do you want a Bud or a Molson?"	+50
"Are you coming to our 50-keg party tonight?"	+75
"What are your SAT scores?"	AVOID
"So what do you think about the international refugee problem?"	AVOID

6. Favorite extracurricular activity of members:

School newspaper	+26
Varsity team sports	+51
Playing frisbee and watching TV	+117
Chess and needlepoint	AVOID

7. How college administration views the house:

Unaware of its existence	−4

Still in good standing but the Dean remains
suspicious   +27
Still on probation since that wild party last
semester   +63
On eternal probation (and for good reasons)
since that incident in 1954 with the hippo
and the Dean's wife   +136
College president and his wife attend daily
house teas   AVOID

8. For sororities and all-female clubs: Type of transportation
   used by members' boyfriends:
   Old family car   −24
   Used car   +34
   New sports car   +74
   Anything requiring exact change   AVOID

9. For fraternities and all-male clubs: Average weight of members' girlfriends:
   Below 120 lbs.   +54
   121–140   +0
   141–160   −43
   More than the combined weight of Nell
   Carter and Mr. T.   AVOID

How FLYERS Balance Their Time Between the Pub and the Library

By now, if you've read the previous chapters in this book, you might be saying to yourself "FLYERS easily balance their time between the pub and the library. Why? Because they just never go to the library." If that's what you're thinking—you're wrong.

FLYERS really do go to the library for four very important reasons:

1. Before the pub opens, it's a super place to talk with friends and even to meet members of the opposite sex.

2. You can take long study breaks (which include going to the pub) and can still count those breaks as part of your library time. No one expects you to study non-stop without taking any breaks.

3. You may sometimes have to tell your parents how many hours you spend in the library—usually this will happen after grades come out. (They'll never think to ask you how many of your hours in the library were actually spent studying. And there's no reason for you to volunteer that information.)

4. Complaining about having to go to the library is an important part of the

experience of going to school. To have any credibility when you complain, you at least have to set foot inside the place.

This simple pie chart gives an indication of how FLYERS balance their free time between the library and their social life. The picture makes it clear that FLYERS spend time in the library. The area shaded in bright orange on the pie chart represents that portion of library time actually spent studying. (Note: This is *not* visible to the naked eye.)

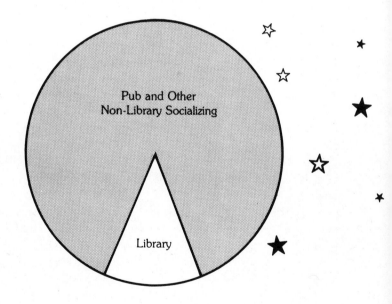

The Eight Commandments
for Avoiding
a Demanding Job

1. Never Accept a Position Where the Last Person to Hold It Died of a Heart Attack
2. Avoid Any Job Which Requires You to Take Orders from Someone Else
3. Accept No Job Which Requires You to Leave Your Home Before Ten in the Morning
4. Don't Perform Any Work That You Are Legally Allowed to Force onto Your Secretary
5. Never Agree to Join a Family Business Until Everyone Is Dead, and

You Can Get Away with Selling It for a Profit
6. Always Quit When It Looks Like You Might Be Fired
7. Refuse to Sign Any Employment Contract That Utilizes Words Like "Deadlines," "Quality Work," "Responsibility," "Perfection," etc.
8. Don't Accept Any Job Where You and Your Boss Have to Work in the Same Building

Favorite Summer Jobs

FLYERS would prefer to put off getting a job, even a summer job, for as long as possible. But when they do decide to work during the summer months, here are their favorite occupations:

LIFEGUARD—A great way to catch some rays and to scope out future prospects (you can tell a lot about someone when you see them in a bathing suit). Only drawback is that you really should know how to swim.

CADDY—There's big money to be made here. But major drawbacks include having to get up before noon on weekends and having to take orders from snotty, rich golfers.

"And then the deranged ax murderer burst into the bunkhouse and hacked up all the young campers in little pieces. The end. Good night everyone. Pleasant dreams."

FAST-FOOD WAITRESS OR WAITER—Fantastic for those who want to lose or gain a lot of weight. You can run yourself ragged or just take it easy and eat up all the profits. You also get to give away free food to friends.

MOVIE USHER OR TICKET TAKER—What a great way to see lots of movies for free, while also keeping track of who comes to the movies with who. You get to keep up on all the local gossip without seeming nosey.

SUMMER INTERN (any industry)—For the ambitious. You get very little work to do, get taken out to great free lunches, and can use a big company's name on your resume.

CAMP COUNSELOR—Ordering around younger campers and telling them horrifying and gory stories before bedtime is a great ego booster.

BARTENDER—An easy way to pick up dates while getting paid. A great head start for FLYERS who plan a career in psychoanalysis or sex counseling.

TELEMARKETING— Sounds really sophisticated but is just selling things over the phone. Since you spend half your life on the telephone anyway, why not get paid for it? Get to insult housewives, business people and others by forcing them to buy products they don't want.

Famous FLYERS
Who Retired by Age 30

Retiring early (yes, amazing as it may seem, working all the way till age 30 is still considered "retiring early") is the ideal of FLYERS. It's not surprising that many well-known FLYERS have retired at a young age. But a brief survey of these individuals reveals that there are several different reasons why they did so.

Some have retired early because they hit their peak before age 30 like Dawn Wells (Mary Ann from "Gilligan's Island"), Max Baer, Jr. (Jethro Clampett from "The

Beverly Hillbillies"), Jerry Mathers (Beaver Cleaver from "Leave It To Beaver"), or Rodney Alan Rippy (child star of popular TV commercials). Unfortunately, it's hard to distinguish people in this group from "has beens" or the chronically unemployed.

Others might be considered in retirement although they have actually never worked at all, like Prince Charles of England (who collects more than half-a-million each year just for being called Your Royal Highness), or Cornelia Guest (the Debutante of the Year, who is a regular at all the chic New York clubs).

But the most favored group are those who could have retired because they've made so much money, like Michael Jackson (who made over $70 million from his *Thriller* album), or Gary Coleman (Arnold on "Dif'rent Strokes") and Emanuel Lewis (Webster on "Webster") who each make $500,000, or anyone featured on "The Lifestyles of the Rich and Famous." But even if you don't make, win, inherit, or steal a million by age 30, the next chapter lists some appropriate FLYERS careers when there's no other choice.

Career Paths That FLYERS Choose When Forced into a Corner

Eventually, it dawns on FLYERS that their fame and fortune will never materialize unless they begin a career. But unlike yuppies, FLYERS don't want to put every waking moment into a job. The time they do spend must be a lot of fun (or at least has to seem like it would be fun). So when full-time employment just can't be avoided any longer, FLYERS decide to become:

1. **ENTREPRENEURS**— Being self-employed sounds exciting and creative—it instantly pegs you as a winner (even if you're not). Greatest benefits: setting your own hours, taking long weekends and vacations, knowing that even if you goof off you can't be fired, and knowing that your boss isn't a jerk.

2. **CELEBRITIES**— Whether you get your cover story in *People* because of acting, singing, dancing, or just being an all-around terrific person, becoming a celebrity is an automatic 24-hour-a-day high. You get to go to the greatest parties, to meet the most interesting people, and to say "No comment" when nosy reporters ask you embarrassing personal questions.

3. **PROFESSIONAL ATHLETE**—You get paid millions of dollars to play your favorite game, and reporters are so excited to interview you they can't even wait for you to get dressed. Very popular athletes also can become celebrities (see above).

4. **WORKING FOR A CELEBRITY OR PRO-FESSIONAL ATHLETE**—Whether you're their agent or you just happen to work as a file clerk for a major corporation which uses a celebrity or professional athlete in its commercials, some of the glamour and excitement of that personality just has to rub off on you.

5. **INTERNATIONAL SO-CIALITE / MILLIONAIRE**—Admittedly, these jobs are very tough to find. But whether you get it by winning the lottery or by inheriting a bundle, being an international socialite means that you don't have to worry that your career will interfere with those essential noontime parties.

6. **WRITER** —Although writing for *People* or even *Time* is more FLYERS-like than writing for *Electronics Age* or *Tiger Beat*, and writing sexy novels is better than writing for encyclopedias, all of these are far superior to becoming a mathematician or the person who cleans the elephant cages at the zoo.

Other plusses: anyone who graduated from sixth grade can write, and you may get to meet celebrities and ask them embarrassing personal questions, which some of them may be stupid enough to answer.

7. **ANYTHING IN THE MOVIE, TV, RECORD, THEATER, OR PUBLISH-ING BUSINESS**—Regardless of how small you may be at Paramount Pictures, NBC, or Motown, you can still tell all your FLYERS friends about their favorite stars (even if you have to make up a few stories). You know you've hit the big time when your office gossip appears the following week in the *National Enquirer*.

8. **EXECUTIVE IN MAR-KETING, ADVERTISING OR PUBLIC RELA-TIONS**—FLYERS love to buy things, so they know how to sell them too—even if it's the most boring (computer hardware or the new Pia Zadora movie), or the most embarrassing (toilet paper or the Osmond family comeback concert) product.

9. **OWNER/MANAGER OF A DANCE CLUB, HEALTH CLUB, OR VACATION RESORT**—With employment like this, you'll have to try hard to distinguish your job from your social life.

10. **WORKING FOR ANY COMPANY THAT MAKES A FAVORITE FLYERS PRODUCT**—You'll never be the life of any party if you bring along the ballistic missile or sewage treatment device which your company manufactures. But see what happens if you bring a jumbo pack of Nestle crunch bars, a case of Jack Daniels, or the floor model Porsche from work.

11. **ANY JOB THAT INVOLVES A LOT OF TRAVEL**—Being able to say, "Tomorrow I'm leaving again for the Virgin Islands, but I still haven't found anyone to use my extra ticket," will make you a very popular person. Examples of these jobs include pilots, flight attendants, and international fugitives.

The Big Picture

FLYERS Tip #4:
How to Avoid Marriage, Homeownership, and Yuppiedom When Things Get Too Serious

A. Marriage—Say goodbye to your free time, your friends, your weekends and your sex life. This is what happens when you get married too early.

Here's how to avoid it:
• When boyfriends get too serious, freak them out by giving yourself a "Mohawk" hairstyle, and telling them that this is your

An easy way to avoid marriage

permanent new look.
- Stop taking baths.
- When she tells you how much she loves you, tell your girlfriend that your last three wives said the same thing.

B. Homeownership—

When your parents suspect that you're making more money than them, you can say "goodbye" to free meals and free rent. They'll insist that you buy your own place if they think you're abusing their hospitality.

Here's how to avoid it:
- Keep up on all of the latest trends and fads so you don't have any money left over for a down payment.
- Even if you're pulling in $50,000, there's no reason why your parents have to know. Keep them in the dark by lying on your tax forms and by dropping a zero from all reported fig-

ures. Even if you go to jail, you'll escape the burden of having to be "out on your own."

C. Yuppiedom—The dis-

ease is spreading fast, but you don't have to become a victim. When you start planning your career and stop going to parties, you'll know that you've fallen into yuppiedom.

Here's how to avoid it:
- In order to make sure your career as a Wall Street banker doesn't get too serious, report to the office with your hair dyed purple and green.
- Gather your squash racket, horn-rimmed glasses, pin-striped business suit, and collection of *New Yorker* magazines and start a bonfire on your front lawn.
- Have your TV antenna rewired so that Public Television shows cannot be transmitted to your home.

Great Moments
in FLYERS History

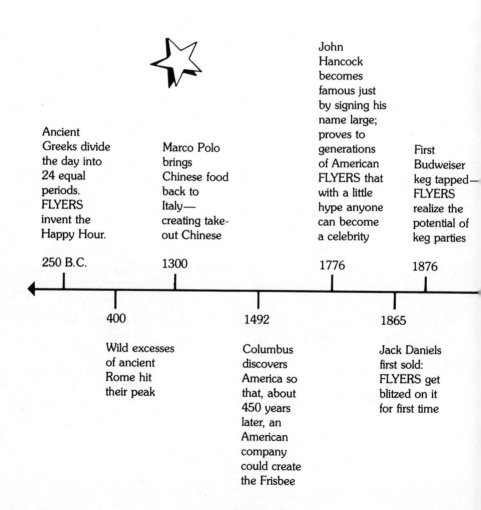

Ancient Greeks divide the day into 24 equal periods. FLYERS invent the Happy Hour.

250 B.C.

Wild excesses of ancient Rome hit their peak

400

Marco Polo brings Chinese food back to Italy— creating take-out Chinese

1300

Columbus discovers America so that, about 450 years later, an American company could create the Frisbee

1492

John Hancock becomes famous just by signing his name large; proves to generations of American FLYERS that with a little hype anyone can become a celebrity

1776

Jack Daniels first sold: FLYERS get blitzed on it for first time

1865

First Budweiser keg tapped— FLYERS realize the potential of keg parties

1876

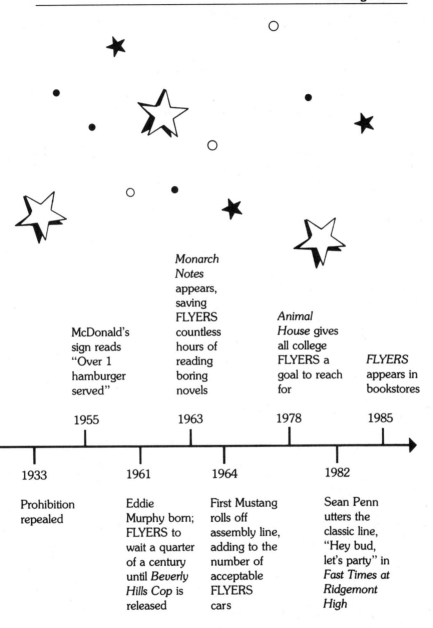

*Monarch
Notes*
appears,
saving
FLYERS
countless
hours of
reading
boring
novels

McDonald's
sign reads
"Over 1
hamburger
served"

*Animal
House* gives
all college
FLYERS a
goal to reach
for

FLYERS
appears in
bookstores

1955   1963   1978   1985

1933   1961   1964   1982

Prohibition
repealed

Eddie
Murphy born;
FLYERS to
wait a quarter
of a century
until *Beverly
Hills Cop* is
released

First Mustang
rolls off
assembly line,
adding to the
number of
acceptable
FLYERS
cars

Sean Penn
utters the
classic line,
"Hey bud,
let's party" in
*Fast Times at
Ridgemont
High*

59

FLYERS' View of the Past

"I think I had pizza and a Bud for dinner last night."

60

Former FLYERS Who Are Expected to Make a Comeback

FLYERS are always doing the unexpected. One of those unexpected activities includes making a comeback once they have lost the attention of their friends and others. Here are some celebrities who consider themselves FLYERS, and here's how we predict each will utilize "FLYERS know-how" in order to make his or her comeback:

1. Doris Day—It's rumored that the "girl next door" will shed her old image by playing a sexy ax-murderess in a rock movie about heroin addicts. (FLYERS will do anything for attention)

2. Vanessa Williams—The grapevine reports that the former Miss America may star in a Broadway play about a teenage nun who starts her own convent. (FLYERS are enterprising)

3. Richard Nixon—Washington gossip has it that the former President may team up with Walter Mondale and take the country by storm in the next Presidential election. (FLYERS never quit)

4. Don Rickles—The Hollywood line claims that the almost-forgotten comedian is about to launch his own line of designer jeans to compete against the less sexy Calvin Klein labels. (FLYERS like to be provocative)

5. Joan Crawford—Many have argued that the famous actress never really died. Rumors say she staged her own funeral just to see what people would write about her. Now, she's billed to star in a hilarious new sitcom this fall, called "Mommie Gets Revenge." (FLYERS have a sense of humor)

6. George Burns—Determined to stay in the public eye, this comedic talent is rumored to be working on a serious new exercise and workout video, with strenuous techniques for people over 90. The new video's clever title: "Breakdancing with George." (FLYERS never grow old)

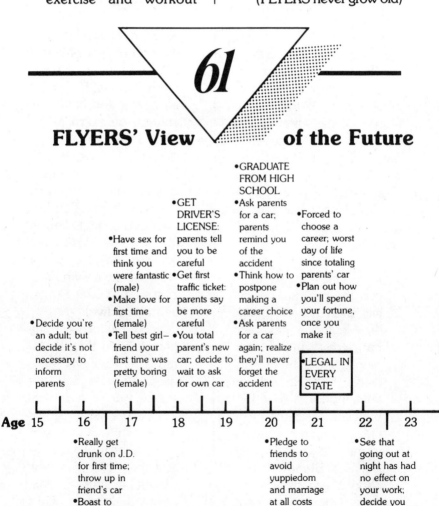

FLYERS' View *61* of the Future

- •GRADUATE FROM HIGH SCHOOL
- •Decide you're an adult; but decide it's not necessary to inform parents
- •Have sex for first time and think you were fantastic (male)
- •Make love for first time (female)
- •Tell best girl-friend your first time was pretty boring (female)
- •GET DRIVER'S LICENSE: parents tell you to be careful
- •Get first traffic ticket: parents say be more careful
- •You total parent's new car; decide to wait to ask for own car
- •Ask parents for a car; parents remind you of the accident
- •Think how to postpone making a career choice
- •Ask parents for a car again; realize they'll never forget the accident
- •Forced to choose a career; worst day of life since totaling parents' car
- •Plan out how you'll spend your fortune, once you make it

•LEGAL IN EVERY STATE

| Age | 15 | 16 | 17 | 18 | 19 | 20 | 21 | 22 | 23 |

- •Really get drunk on J.D. for first time; throw up in friend's car
- •Boast to friends about having sex (male)

- •Pledge to friends to avoid yuppiedom and marriage at all costs

- •See that going out at night has had no effect on your work; decide you need to reform and spend more time partying

154

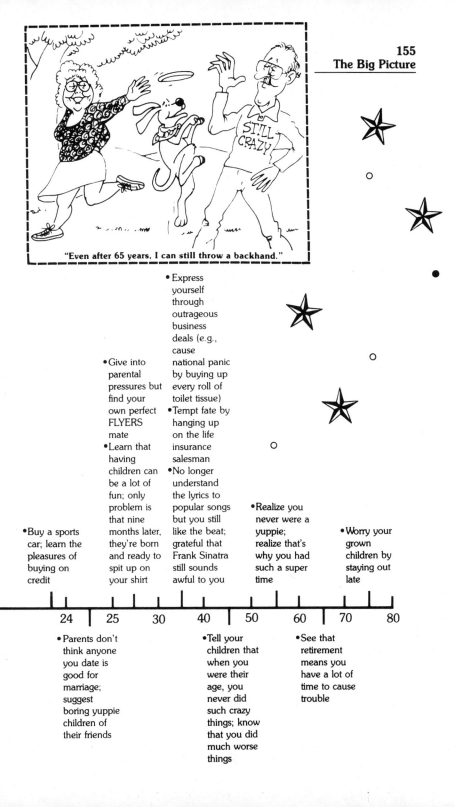

"Even after 65 years, I can still throw a backhand."

• Express yourself through outrageous business deals (e.g., cause national panic by buying up every roll of toilet tissue)

• Give into parental pressures but find your own perfect FLYERS mate

• Tempt fate by hanging up on the life insurance salesman

• Learn that having children can be a lot of fun; only problem is that nine months later, they're born and ready to spit up on your shirt

• No longer understand the lyrics to popular songs but you still like the beat; grateful that Frank Sinatra still sounds awful to you

• Realize you never were a yuppie; realize that's why you had such a super time

• Buy a sports car; learn the pleasures of buying on credit

• Worry your grown children by staying out late

| 24 | 25 | 30 | 40 | 50 | 60 | 70 | 80 |

• Parents don't think anyone you date is good for marriage; suggest boring yuppie children of their friends

• Tell your children that when you were their age, you never did such crazy things; know that you did much worse things

• See that retirement means you have a lot of time to cause trouble

62

The Official FLYERS Final Exam

You've taken final exams all your life, so why stop now? Just to make sure you've paid close attention to the details of FLYERS lifestyle (and to save yourself from future embarrassment), test yourself with the following:

1. Who is credited with discovering America?
   a) Joan Collins
   b) Jackie Collins
   c) Barnabas Collins
   d) Christopher Columbus

2. The sex life of which famous individual has never been called into question?
   a) Boy George
   b) Michael Jackson
   c) Tennis star Dr. Renee Richards
   d) E.T.

3. Which of the following is a favorite FLYERS TV actor?
   a) Jack Daniels
   b) Johnny Walker
   c) Tom Collins
   d) Tom Selleck

4. In which activity does "Dr. J" specialize?
   a) gynecology
   b) brain surgery
   c) pediatrics
   d) basketball

5. Which of the following songs was written by the great composer Johannes Brahms?
   a) "The Glamorous Life"
   b) "Girls Just Wanna Have Fun"
   c) "Wake Me Up Before You Go-Go"
   d) Symphony No. 4 in E minor

6. Which historical novel was written by Leo Tolstoy?
   a) *Fast Times at Ridgemont High*
   b) *Valley of the Dolls*
   c) *Real Men Don't Eat Quiche*
   d) *War and Peace*

7. What famous designer is credited with creating the MX missile?
   a) Gloria Vanderbilt
   b) Calvin Klein
   c) Ralph Lauren
   d) some physicist from M.I.T.

8. Which Oscar-winning movie chronicled the life of a famous, outspoken leader from India?
   a) *Flashdance*
   b) *Repo Man*
   c) *Desperately Seeking Susan*
   d) *Gandhi*

Answers:

The probable answer to all questions is (d), except for #7. It would take too much time to find the answer to that question, and if you're a true FLYER you probably don't care anyway.

63

The FLYERS
Code of Honor

1. I will not worry about the future.
2. I will not worry about my past.
3. I will drop the word *guilt* from my vocabulary.
4. I will buy what makes me happy.
5. I will not make friends with pushy people.
6. I will walk away from situations which threaten my ego.
7. I will always work my hardest—when I feel like it.
8. I will use up all my vacation days.
9. I will learn to stop saving for the future.
10. I will reach Success... because I deserve it.

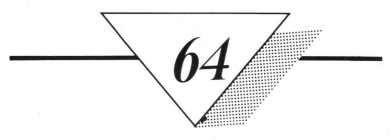

Become One of the Official FLYERS

Would you like to become one of the Official FLYERS (5 to be chosen from each state) and be part of our upcoming national survey of young people?

Just fill out this form and tell us—in 20 words or less—what makes you part of the FLYERS generation.

Mail by November 15, 1985 to FLYERS
                                      c/o Simon & Schuster
                                      Publicity Dept.
                                      1230 Avenue of the Americas
                                      New York, N.Y. 10020

Name_____ Age_____

Address_____
          _____
School_____

I'm one of the FLYERS because_____
_____

Photocopies of this page cannot be honored.

159

ABOUT THE AUTHORS

Lawrence Graham is the author of eight books, including *Conquering College Life*. A graduate of Princeton University, and a student at Harvard Law School, he is a partner and co-founder of FLYERS Consulting, a firm which advises corporations on how to sell to the 15- to 25-year-old age group. In addition to holding a position in the White House during a previous administration, Graham has been hailed by *Mademoiselle* magazine as one of "The 10 Most Interesting Young Men in America."

Lawrence Hamdan is a graduate of Princeton University and a student in the joint program of Harvard Law School and Harvard Business School. In addition to his experience in investment banking on Wall Street, Hamdan has edited three books and is a partner and co-founder of FLYERS Consulting.